PRAISE

"Imagine what the world would be like if everyone enjoyed true financial freedom? What if we (you) didn't have to work for money but could dedicate your time and brilliance to purpose? In Financial Freedom Accelerated 2x-10x Faster, Shauy not only inspires with the promise of financial freedom but offers a formula to achieve it."

-- Professor Kaihan Krippendorff, MBA
Founder of Outthinker, Keynote Speaker, Board Member, McKinsey Alumnus
Author of "Outthink the Competition: How a New Generation of Strategists See Options Others Ignore"
United States

"A must-read book. Sidney Shauy is not only a math whizz but an extremely experienced investor, determined to help people achieve financial stability. A game changer, unique and impactful! For a world in deep transformation, the path to financial freedom is more complex. Sidney empowers individuals not only to plan but also to execute on transformative investments. Really, a must-read book!"

-- Gabriela Herculano, MBA
CEO of iClima Earth
London Stock Exchange-traded ETF's and stock indexes on renewable energy and climate change adaptation
London, Singapore

"In this ingenious book, in simple and everyday language, Sidney Shauy makes us rethink what we believe about investments and gives us the tools needed for reaching financial independence."

-- Lisandra Flynn, Esq.
Partner, Lopes Pinto Nagasse Business Law

International Tax, Corporate, and Succession Planning
United States

"Sidney Shauy does a great job giving his insights on investing and I think this is a great book for anyone to learn investing and improving their financial freedom. As a CPA, I think it's really important to have this knowledge as I have seen many clients not having the proper knowledge to manage their money."

-- Vincenzo Villamena, CPA
CEO of Online Taxman
Author of "US Taxes for Americans Abroad: The Easy Guide to Saving Money"
United States

"Sidney Shauy is one of those few people who make the world better! Working in the financial and real estate markets in several countries, he managed to maintain tenderness and empathy when treating people and meeting what they need from his experience and wisdom. Rare are those who achieve this and still be happy, always with a smile and enchantment. Sidney is unique! Congratulations for the book!!"

-- Heitor Kuser, MBA, Esq.
CEO of Kuser International
International Advisor to the Brazilian National Real Estate Board
Brazil

"A book that will help people, simply put. Thank you, Sidney, and congrats again."

-- Michael Buono, MBA
CEO, Mulberry Development and Construction Group
CEO of New York Renaissance Group

"Many people know the concept of revenues, but have you been taking full advantage of its power? Is money dripping between your checking accounts without you even being aware? How many years were wasted by not building assets for your financial freedom? Or by choosing bad investing decisions? This book is intended to provide general and specific information for educational purposes related how to boot your economic independence. Sidney Shauy who has years of experience in these financial aspects has developed a book with clear language, common sense and a very define practical rules in order to accelerate your economic independency."

-- Professor Guillermo Monroy, PhD
Business School Faculty, IEB
JP Morgan alumnus, ex-Head of Trading at BBVA, Board Member
Madrid, London, New York
** Personal endorsement; not by employers*

"With characteristic clarity and simplicity Mr. Shauy proposes a system for personal portfolio management that is fit for the challenges of the new age of finance. With online support modules and resources, his unique approach will be of great value to a broad range of investors seeking expedited financial freedom. Two thumbs up."

- Rodrigo Espírito-Santo, MBA
Managing Director, Torino Capital LLC
Investment bank industry veteran: Emerging Markets Rates, FX, Credit, Derivatives
United States
** Personal endorsement; not by employer*

"This book is exactly what you would expect from an engineer, raised in an Emerging Market economy, and with a long career in the banking industry in NY: solve your wealth generation speed problem. Sidney writes in a straightforward, no-nonsense way, breaking down the path to success into baby steps that anyone can understand. Just by opening this book, the reader has already stepped into the path of his/her financial independence, many times faster!"

-- Shinishiro Fukui, MSc

Senior Partner, Stratton Capital Investment Advisory
Fixed Income Strategist and Portfolio Manager, industry veteran
United States, Japan, UK, Brazil
** Personal endorsement; not by employer*

"Everyone has a past, a present and a future, for as long it lasts. Satisfying the hunger for knowledge is, therefore, inevitable, as no one wants to repeat past mistakes, remain indecisive in the present and, worse, reap bad results in the future. Every opportunity to learn, develop and make the right decisions must be used wisely and thoroughly. Financial Freedom Accelerated 2x-10x Faster, by Sidney Shauy, MBA, proposes the rare opportunity to enrich the hunger for knowledge in clear language and nonetheless in a comprehensive way, hoping to give to the reader paths of avoiding the mistakes committed in the past, empowering the reader with wise decisions in the present, and creating best conditions to obtain good results be reaped in the future."

-- Antonio Roberto Catalano Junior, LLM
Managing Partner, Analytic Partners Capital Management LLC
Legal Structuring, Corporations and Business Associations Law
United States and Brazil

"Thank you, Sidney, for providing the template for Financial Freedom. It's easy to follow and within reach of everyone."

-- Robert Kauffman
Director, MassMutual Life Insurance Company Tri State
Estate Planning and Business Planning, industry veteran
United States
** Personal endorsement; not by employer*

FINANCIAL FREEDOM

ACCELERATED
2x – 10x FASTER

A Multi-Asset Class Step by Step Formula

- 1st Edition -

SIDNEY SHAUY, MBA

PALLAS VESTA
PUBLISHING CO. LLC

Published by Pallas Vesta Publishing Company LLC, New Jersey, USA

PALLAS VESTA
PUBLISHING CO. LLC

Pallas Vesta Publishing Company LLC
New Jersey, NJ – United States of America

Discounts for bulk sales are available. Please contact us by email below.

SIDNEY
SHAUY

Financial Freedom
Accelerated 2x-10x

ISBN: 978-1-960691-02-6 (eBook)
ISBN: 978-1-960691-03-3 (Paperback)
ISBN: 978-1-960691-04-0 (Hardcover)

First Edition: 2023

www.acceleratedfinancialfreedom.com

Printed in the United States of America. Editing and proofreading by Becky Ross Michael. Cover design by Pallas Vesta Publishing Company LLC

Financial Freedom [fīˈnan(t)SHəl,ˈfrēdəm] n. condition in which a person, family or household no longer depends on the fruits of their labor to cover all expenses to maintain their chosen standard of living. Financial freedom can be achieved after an initial investment of time, effort, and money produced sufficient residual income continually into the future.

DEDICATION

This book is dedicated to all the honest, hardworking men and women, who have a dream for a better future, free of financial worries.

It is dedicated to individual investors, who are trying their best to figure out what to do in a challenging economy and markets.

I also wish to make a special dedication to all workers who are feeling stressed because of job insecurity from constant threats of being laid off, suffering the physical and mental burnout from a toxic workplace, or simply feeling overworked and underpaid.

This book is dedicated to everyone who believes in themselves, even in the face of adversity, and never loses hope that they will realize their dreams.

You are true heroes and the source of my inspiration.

SPECIAL THANKS

To my family, for their unconditional love and support, always
To my parents and grandparents, my eternal gratitude
To my mentors, for their wisdom and inspiration

GENERAL DISCLAIMER

While a great deal of care has been taken to provide accurate, informative, and helpful material on the subjects addressed in the book, neither the publisher nor the author is responsible for any errors and omissions, or the results obtained from the use of this information. The book contains ideas and opinions of the author. The strategies outlined in the book may not be suitable for every person under any circumstances, and they are not warranted or guaranteed to produce any particular results. The book is intended to provide general information for educational purposes only.

The book is sold with the understanding that neither the author nor the publisher is engaged in providing legal, business, financial, investment, tax, accounting, securities or any other professional advice. The author is not a licensed advisor. The reader should always consult with their own trusted and licensed professional advisors before adopting any of the suggested strategies in the book or drawing inferences from them. The contents of this book are provided "as is," without guarantees of accuracy, completeness, or timeliness regarding the results obtained from their use. The reader assumes full responsibility for the use of this information and uses it at their own risk. Neither the author nor the publisher will be liable for any direct, indirect, special, incidental, consequential, or punitive damages of any nature. In no event, whatsoever, will the author, Sidney Shauy, nor the publisher, Pallas Vesta Publishing Company LLC, their related companies, partners, agents, employees, associates, service providers, or their employees, be liable to readers or anyone for any decision or action taken in reliance on the contents of this book and its consequences. The information and all figures in this book that were accurate at the time of the writing may become inaccurate or outdated with the passage of time and by changes in the economy and markets. New laws and taxes may be enacted. Figures, including prices and rates, and assumptions are not guaranteed and are subject to change at any time. Any slights against individuals, groups, organizations, or companies are unintentional. Models used in the book are based on assumptions, which may or may not apply to everyone, and are subject to errors, omissions, and change. All models are simplifications of reality and must be understood as such. As in all models, assumptions, and numerical examples in the book, it has been stressed multiple times that individual results vary based on a wide range of factors related to each person's unique set of circumstances, needs, goals, quality of execution of strategies, in addition to uncontrollable factors, such as the moment and status of the economy and markets.

About the Author

Sidney Shauy is an analytics-driven investor and entrepreneur, who designed solutions combining financial instruments, real estate, and insurance. The author has over 30 years of combined experience with real estate investing, insurance structuring, and world financial markets in leading global banks such as Citigroup, Morgan Stanley, Lloyds Bank, ABN Amro, Bilbao Vizcaya, in New York, Hong Kong, and Sao Paulo.

Fluent in 4 languages, he earned an MBA degree from the Wharton School of the University of Pennsylvania

https://engineering-finance.medium.com

https://www.linkedin.com/in/sidneyshauy/

https://www.acceleratedfinancialfreedom.com/

https://www.engineering-fnance.com/afff

Table of Contents

PREFACE – A SPECIAL NOTE TO OUR INTERNATIONAL AUDIENCE

It was a great pleasure to learn from the 1st Edition that it would have a wide international acceptance. So much so that I decided to add this special note to our global audience.

All the concepts and ideas in the book are universal and can be applied everywhere in the world, although it's been written in the United States with examples and discussions taken from the American context.

Slight differences may exist from country to country. Still, every country has a stock market, a real estate market, small businesses, life insurance, and other forms of investments and risk management instruments. The author himself has had work and life experiences in many countries.

The four principles making the core of the Accelerated Financial Freedom Formula™ that will accelerate your journey to financial freedom should certainly work anywhere in the world.

INTRODUCTION

How do you speed up a journey from point A to point B? There are only two possible ways:

- Increase your speed or
- shorten the travel distance

The Accelerated Financial Freedom Formula™ (the AFFF) aims to do **both** for your financial freedom.

What is financial freedom? It seems to mean different things to different people these days because the expression has been too overused. Many people are led to believe only the very rich can be financially free. Is it true? No, not necessarily, and you will find out why in the book. Ultimately, you want the freedom that money, or finance, can provide you.

If you are interested in financial freedom or a comfortable early retirement, you may have read many articles and books or perhaps even joined a FIRE (Financial Independence Retire Early) movement. But this book is different, and the concept of the Accelerated Financial Freedom Formula™ (AFFF) goes one important step further.

To start, the AFFF adds one crucial variable most popular financial freedom methods ignore: the T I M E dimension. This makes these methods highly inefficient and penalizes you, the user. Even for a small retirement income, they typically require you to save over a million dollars, don't they? For a wealthy or high-income earner, it's doable. But what about everyone else? Well, some of you may still do it, but you are required to live frugally for years, if not decades, on an aggressive savings regime. Can you see there is a serious problem? The most commonly recommended solution to speed up the process is by asking you to work side hustles to increase your income to save more. Honestly, how efficient do you think that is? If you have tried it before, I believe this will resonate with you. For me, it's clear that the problem is not exactly the investment assets (the what), but the methods (the how). Fortunately for you, I hope, the AFFF will help you **achieve financial freedom much faster than this and with less money required**.

As an ex-Wall Street banker in 4 countries for 20 years, with an MBA degree from Wharton and later self-employed as a real estate syndicator-investor and entrepreneur for another 10 years, I had the opportunity to get myself exposed to challenges in multiple fields, ranging from financial markets to real estate and insurance. I developed the AFFF over many years from my own experience on the battlefield, after many trials and errors. I was just looking for ways to get to retire early myself. This happened before I had the chance to read a single book about financial freedom. Thus, I was never influenced by other people's ideas and developed my methods independently from existing schools of thought.

The first problem with existing methods, in my view, is that people just follow existing conventions. To create income and wealth, some of you will embrace Wall Street ideas, investing in stocks, bonds, mutual funds, and tax-deferred plans (e.g. 401k, etc.). Others will take the real estate investing route. There are very few people who are equally engaged in BOTH. Why? It's simply because they belong to separate industries – the financial and the real estate industries. This is a purely human convention and a human-created limitation. I believe we should not be constrained by existing conventions, nor by the current system design and industry interests. In my view, we should access the broadest array of options possible. Think about it. If you are going to war, would you go with a single weapon or with as many weapons as possible and know how and when to deploy each weapon depending on the battlefield conditions? The Accelerated Financial Freedom Formula™ (AFFF) is based on these 4 principles:

- **Multi-asset approach**: a two-stage strategy with multiple asset types to maximize production of growth and income.
- **Timing investments to the context**: strategically choose assets depending on the state of the economy and market cycles. No static or simplistic rules of thumb.
- **Borrow the strength of a greater force**: don't rely on your own financial strength alone. Leverage with 2 types of OPM ("Other People's Money"): OPM/E (OPM from external sources) and OPM/I (OPM from internal sources).
- **Money Booster**: optimize the way you use money, and you will maximize compound interest, reduce lost opportunity costs, and stop money leaks from eroding your wealth.

In the book, I will prove to you mathematically why the AFFF can accelerate your journey to financial freedom 2x - 10x faster than mainstream traditional methods. This book isn't about just mindset or general advice. The AFFF will provide a 9-step guide/checklist so that everyone can actually implement the method on their own or seek further help and financial education (mentorship and workshops available).

I commend you for taking this important and serious step towards your financial freedom journey by reading this book. Your time is very valuable, and I assume you are a busy person. While the financial industry developed methods that are more "done for you" type of solutions, in contrast, real estate pros developed methods that typically demand a lot of time from you to learn and implement. Nevertheless, the best method for a busy person lies somewhere in between, not on the extremes. The best solution is twofold: get yourself educated quickly and create a system. With a system, complicated things become easy, you streamline your execution, and save time. A system created under the AFFF framework will put the control in your own hands, giving you choices and maximum flexibility to fit your own schedule and pace. One of the goals of the AFFF is to help you create your own system. I believe that good methods must adapt to you, the user, your needs and circumstances, and not the other way around, like most methods out there.

I will leave you with this last thought before you read the book. I believe that to be successful, we need to think out of the box, to extend our vision beyond typically accepted norms, and to use the system in our favor, instead of being used by it or being constrained by it. Below, you will see an excerpt from a TED Talk titled "Why the majority is always wrong" by Paul Rulkens, author and specialist in high-performance. I hope it will be an eye opener for you as much as it was for me.

"In 1942, Albert Einstein was teaching at Oxford University, and one day, he just gave an exam of physics to his senior class of physics students. He was walking on the campus with his assistant, and all of a sudden, the assistant looked at Albert Einstein and said:

- *"Dr. Einstein, this exam which you just gave to the senior class of physics students, isn't that exactly the same exam you gave to exactly the same class one year ago?"*
- *"Yeah, yeah," replied Albert Einstein, "it's exactly the same."*
- *"But Dr. Einstein, how could you possibly do that?" the assistant asked.*
- *"Well," said Einstein, "the answers have changed."*

The answers have changed. In other words, what was true for 1942 is even more true today. We live in a world where the questions might be the same, but the answers have changed. In other words, what has got you here will no longer get you there. And if you want to have results that you've never had before, well, you need to start doing things you've never done before. (…)

If you do what everyone else is doing, you're not distinguishing yourself, and you're probably stuck. We know that 3% of people can achieve extraordinary results. Each of you can become part of those 3%, by deciding as of today to break your industry standards and to break your industry norms. The alternative, of course, is that you become part of the 97%, who, in the end, works for the 3%. As of today, that choice is completely yours. Thank you very much."

Financial Freedom 2x to 10x Faster

The Accelerated Financial Freedom Formula ™

CHAPTER 1

1. Becoming financially free 2x-10x faster with less money required

Is this even possible?

YES! You heard me right, and that's why I decided to write this book. **Virtually anyone can become financially free 2x-10x faster with less money (or savings) required than traditional methods**. For example, for someone who, by traditional means, would take decades to build enough assets to generate enough income to match their expenses or lifestyle, he/she may achieve financial freedom in a much shorter time period with less money required by following the Accelerated Financial Freedom Formula ™ (AFFF).

What is financial freedom?

Imagine living a life not needing to worry about money (or the lack thereof). It's freedom to live a life worth living, do things you love, spend more time with your loved ones. It's freedom to choose a career you love, regardless of pay, and work only with people you like. Or the complete freedom to pursue your passion and dreams even if these are unpaid or low pay activities. Back to the real world, the only solution to this ideal world boils down to one word: income.

Imagine if you had a separate stream of passive income, independent from your active income source (from work), in an amount sufficient to pay all your bills and living expenses. You may quit your job if you choose because all your expenses will be covered. Would you be financially free? Yes, money is not everything in life, but it gives you choices and can buy you freedom.

But what, exactly, is financial freedom? The expression has been abusively overused to mean a lot of different things, but according to the most serious authors, financial freedom is achieved when you gain the ability to **generate enough residual passive income to offset all your living expenses**. Note that I said "residual" and "passive income." This simply means an activity that **after an initial investment of time, effort, and money, will produce income for you continually into the future**.

For example, the income you receive from your work salary does not qualify as passive or residual income. This is active income because you are simply trading your time, skills, and energy for money. Even if you make a lot of it. For example, a highly paid doctor or attorney may be rich, but they're not financially free because if they don't show up for work the next day, they won't get paid.

Consider some super-talented people you know who worked for a few years to create patents (inventions), royalties and copyrights (music, movies, books, etc.) that will pay them and their descendants passive income continually for the rest of their lives. These people worked hard to make their creations initially and only once. Then they received passive and residual income for the rest of their lives. The obvious question then becomes: what if I'm not a super-talented musician, inventor, or movie star?

Thankfully, there is another way for the rest of us, and that is through strategic investments. Simply speaking, it's using your money to work for you 24/7, 365 days per year, even while you are sleeping or gone fishing. Instead of trading your valuable time for money, your money (your investments) should work hard to generate the income you need to sustain the lifestyle you desire. That is financial freedom, the holy grail to break yourself free from active work income (e.g., salary, etc.) dependency.

An entrepreneur, who worked hard to build a business that can be run later **without him/her**, can also be financially free. You must have realized by now that financial freedom is usually achieved by means of strategic investments where you will commit some time, employ your skills, and invest some money to build assets **one time** that will produce income for you, preferably passively, for the rest of your life. Such assets can be a multitude of instruments strategically selected and invested, which I will discuss extensively throughout the book. The income these investments generate must cover all your living expenses and desired lifestyle before you declare yourself financially free. In summary, what does and does not lead you to financial freedom:

- **Work for wages, commissions, etc.** = You trade your time, skills, efforts for money. You must work continuously for the money. No work, no money: this is NOT financial freedom.
- **Patents, royalties, copyrights from creative talent (inventors, artists, etc.)** = You worked initially but receive income in perpetuity: YES, it leads to financial freedom.
- **Entrepreneurship** = You worked hard initially to create a business with a profitable system and became an absentee owner: you receive income from the business even if you don't work there anymore or devote very little time to it: YES, it leads to financial freedom.

- **Investment** = You invested money, time, and efforts initially to set up investments. You make adjustments from time to time. Your investments work for you generating income continually with the least time demand as possible: YES, it leads to financial freedom.

The choice is yours. What will be your choice? Entrepreneurship and investment are the only suitable choices for most of us, who are not inventors or artists. This book will focus mostly on investments, but also on one type of entrepreneurship, that of a special type of small business that may run for an absentee owner.

Financial freedom is the power to switch the nature of your income from an active income source (you working for your money) to passive income sources (your money working for you)

Finally, because financial freedom frees you from needing to trade your time and energy for money (e.g., work for salary, etc.), you essentially win your precious time back.

Is this even possible? Absolutely. Millions of people around the world have achieved financial freedom one way or another. They are living proof it is very possible and there are many roads that lead to Rome, in this case, financial freedom. Some use real estate. Some use financial markets such as stocks and bonds. They were all able to achieve their financial freedom. The only problem is how long did they take? Years? A few decades, more likely? Some of them did it faster because they had a high income from work or started with a large amount of savings, but what if you don't have as much? Have they had to make great sacrifices living below their means for a very long period of time? Or perhaps, they got there faster because they had rich parents? The unfortunate thing for most people is that, for obvious reasons, apparently only high earners and the wealthy can do it fast. Traditional ways don't help those with more modest means: for them, it may take decades, an entire lifetime, or they may never achieve financial freedom. No wonder so few people even believe in financial freedom. They think it may have worked for others; but for themselves, it is just an impossible dream.

I hope the AFFF will change this unfair situation and enable more people to achieve financial freedom faster and with less money required. The AFFF is not reinventing the wheel, and it is definitely NOT a get rich quick scheme or an insanely high return (but risky) investment. The AFFF is not an investment that will return x, y, or z; rather, the AFFF is a method. The AFFF intends to help make the most out of your hard-earned dollars and to work more efficiently for you than traditional methods. As you will discover reading the book, the AFFF was developed to optimize the way things are done to seriously accelerate your journey to financial freedom.

What is your most valuable asset?

Have you ever thought about this? Some people will say it's their money or other valuable physical assets. Others will say it's their education, experience, or another 'priceless' intangible. Some will even say it's their kids or other loved ones. But the reality is that T I M E is the most valuable asset we are given since birth. Time is a finite resource for each and every one of us, no matter whether you are Elon Musk or Jimmy Musk. Our clocks are ticking at the same rate since birth. How we spend our time on Earth is up to us. Do you prefer to spend most of your time working in something that doesn't make you happy just for the money or working in something you love that doesn't pay you as much? Do you prefer to spend more time with your co-workers or with your loved ones? Do you want to spend your life building your dreams or building someone else's dreams?

Financial freedom will give you back the right to choose what to do with your TIME.

That's why you should not only seek financial freedom; but you should also do your best to accelerate it like there is no tomorrow. Wasting time postponing your dreams not knowing what or how to do something is understandable and excusable. But now that you will know how to do it with a proven method, not taking immediate action becomes foolish. If your personal circumstances (e.g. low savings rate, low wages, etc.) would only permit you to achieve financial freedom in 20, 30, or 40 years through traditional ways, you have even more reasons to consider the AFFF to accelerate your way to financial freedom.

Remember, **time is finite** and **the most valuable asset** you have. Don't waste it. Don't sell it cheap to some capitalist to exploit your skills, time, and efforts. Use them to build your financial freedom instead of theirs. Make every second of your life journey on Earth be worth living, for your own sake.

Do you need to be rich to be financially free?

One of the main reasons people believe financial freedom to be out of their reach is that they think one must be rich, very rich, to be financially free. This is not true. I know this too well because I held the exact same beliefs since childhood. In reality, you don't need to be rich to be financially free. Conversely, a rich person may not necessarily be financially free.

Consider these three very different people:

Images: Courtesy of Unsplash, inspired from example given by Strongbrook

The first is a doctor making $20,000 a month from his medical practice. The second is a businessman making $10,000 a month. The third is a teacher making $5,000 a month from her wages as an educator. She has 10 small real estate investments cashing her $9,000 a month. Note that neither the doctor who has a high salary, nor the businessman, who is technically a millionaire, are financially free. If either of these two gentlemen decided not to work anymore, their income would stop, and they would have to tap into their wealth to pay for living expenses. The only person in this example to be financially free is the teacher, even though she makes the lowest income from work among the three of them. If she decided not to work as a teacher anymore, her properties will continue to cashflow to her.

As you can see, **income is the key for financial freedom**. **Only pure income can efficiently offset expenses.** Being wealthy is not a pre-condition for financial freedom most of us are led to believe. It is not an absolute requirement. However, wealth does help a great deal and speeds up the process. Having money naturally puts you closer to financial freedom, no doubt about that. For someone with modest means to reach financial freedom, it will take longer and more effort. But the good news is that the AFFF was developed precisely for those who aren't wealthy already also to have a chance. With a more efficient method you will learn about by reading this book, everyone should benefit. That is the reason I developed the AFFF and very purpose of this book.

Why and who should pursue financial freedom?

Financial freedom should be a goal for **everyone**, all ages, genders, and walks of life. But certain groups of folks are in more pressing and urgent need of financial freedom:

Salaried Workers – The structure of the corporate hierarchy is a pyramid. This means that fewer and fewer people will make it up the corporate ladder. It is so by design. As a result, the vast majority will never make above a certain pay grade and will either quit, be fired, or get stuck. The job market is also cruel to those reaching a certain age, not to mention those in minority groups. Financial freedom will certainly help these people at any stage in their careers with extra income, but above all, give them a priceless sense of financial security, regardless of their pay grade at their companies. The earlier they start working on their financial freedom plans, the better. Time passes fast, and ideally, financial freedom should be achieved before age becomes a problem in the job market for their line of work.

Another huge problem in the corporate world is the incredible number of people that are very dissatisfied with their jobs, be it because of their managers, their pay, their work environment, their daily commute, their lack of advancement opportunities, their feeling of unfair treatment due to office politics, or all of the above. But without passive residual income on the side to pay their bills, they are essentially stuck, shackled to a job from which they derive no satisfaction. If this feels like you, you are certainly not alone. I was in this huge group too, until I was able to achieve my own financial freedom and left my 20-year corporate career early for a much better lifestyle. I never looked back. I also work for myself, doing only things that make me happy, and with only the people I like. The freedom I enjoy today is priceless. My only regret is that I hadn't done it (or found a better way to do it) much earlier.

Self-Employed Professionals and Start-up Entrepreneurs – Self-employed professionals enjoy flexibility and don't have a boss, but the downside is the unpredictability and irregularity of their income. Non-salaried sales professionals who depend on commissions suffer from the same problem. People with entrepreneurial veins want to venture out on their own starting a new business. The first few years of any new business are the hardest, and often new entrepreneurs don't make any money. For all of these folks, financial freedom will provide income while the business is still unprofitable, but above all, it will give them peace of mind to pursue their dreams.

People with Highly Satisfying but Low or No Pay Jobs – People who dedicate themselves to their passions, such as art, social causes, public service, clergy, etc. often find themselves in careers that may not pay them well enough to cover all their bills or to live a desired lifestyle. Money problems cause major life unhappiness. Financial freedom will help them bridge the gap and give them peace of mind to continue their work without money worries.

Retirees and Pre-Retirees Without Retirement Security – Unfortunately, a large number of retirees are living below preretirement living standards and feel scared about the very real possibility of outliving their retirement savings. Traditional financial planning has failed so many people. Static and simplistic formulas such as the 4% Rule often fail because assumptions are often proven to be too optimistic. Social Security running dangerously near insolvency may potentially cut benefits pushing millions of beneficiaries into poverty. A very large number of pre-retirees, even folks in their 40's and 50's, are increasingly concerned they won't be able to accumulate a sufficiently large nest egg by the time they retire to have a comfortable retirement. As 2000, 2008, 2020, and 2022 bear markets (i.e., markets in which prices are consistently falling) have shown, stock and bond-dependent plans such as 401k's and balanced portfolios are exposed to volatility that can make decades of retirement savings evaporate quickly, in just a matter of weeks. Then you have to question the all-cherished tax-deferral benefit of government-sponsored plans (e.g. 401k, IRA, etc.): is it a smart choice to defer taxes if future tax rates are likely to be higher? Retirees and pre-retirees don't have much margin for error, especially if they don't have millions in their retirement accounts and elsewhere.

Workers at Risk of being Laid Off – While everyone is exposed to the risk of being the next to receive the "pink slip," some workers are at higher risk than others. Someone who's past a certain age and have been passed for promotion many times must be on high alert. People with high compensation in companies with declining financials should also be careful. Workers in some functions that can be replaced by automation are another high-risk group. I hope you are not in any of these high-risk situations, but in any event, it would be smart to prepare your finances, and if possible, start working on your financial freedom as soon as possible. As the quote goes, "*…the time to repair the roof is when the sun is shining" (John F. Kennedy, former U.S. president).*

Young Folks and, Heck, Everyone Else! – Regardless of your personal reason to pursue financial freedom, the AFFF may be not only your best shot at achieving financial freedom, but also at an accelerated pace, given your own unique circumstances. For younger people, it may be even more powerful because TIME is definitely on their side, more so than older folks. But time ticks fast, and if you procrastinate, your advantage is gone.

Financial freedom can certainly help everyone avoid the worst and bring them more financial and retirement security sooner, without the fear of ever outliving their life savings.

CHAPTER 2

2. Mainstream traditional methods may work: but at what cost?

Yes, many traditional methods do allow people to achieve financial freedom. I'm in no way contesting that. Some do work. But the question is, at what cost? How much money are people required to save? How long will the journey take until they finally achieve their financial freedom? The long time it takes is a big cost to you, is it not? Why do so many people simply not believe they will ever reach financial freedom with traditional methods?

First, let me clarify what I mean by traditional methods. Unless there are secret methods out there that I have no clue about, the only methods I have seen and heard time and time again can be grouped in only two major but different industry camps: the financial markets camp and the real estate camp. Again, this is because the system is fragmented: the financial industry and real estate industry exist in two separate worlds. The financial industry proposed an easy and convenient "done for you" solution, and the real estate industry proposed a very different solution. Let's examine both methods:

Financial freedom methods based on financial markets

The first major method is popular with FIRE, Wall Street, and white-collar folks in general. It's generally based on some variation of creating balanced portfolios (e.g., 60/40 or investing 60% in stocks and 40% in bonds) to grow your savings, and after you reach retirement day, taking 4% annual withdrawals for income (the famous 4% rule), until the day you die. Whatever is left, if there is anything left, you leave to your heirs as inheritance.

I don't know about you, but I see many problems with this approach. First, it's based on too many assumptions; the most troubling is that the stock market will have to consistently return above 4% or else your portfolio may be exhausted. Well, we all know this is not an ironclad assumption. There also is a real risk that people may outlive their nest eggs (the so-called longevity risk). But the biggest problem, in my view, is the amount of capital required to retire and the time to get there. It was definitely a method created to help those already wealthy or with high incomes to retire comfortably, and I highly doubt it would work for middle-class families. Under this method, if you aren't rich with high income, you will most likely take many decades to get your financial freedom. For those at the lower end of the spectrum, not even their entire lifetimes would be enough. For example, for someone wanting $40,000 per year income, which is not a lot of money, you would need to accumulate $1 million as the target capital, if you follow the 4% rule. Target capital = 25x target income, under the 4% rule. Now, even if you do manage to get there, you will have to pray that every year the stock market or another type of investment you chose will never grow less than 4% until the day you die. If it didn't for a year, you will need subsequent years to make up for the difference. Plus, of course, assuming there is no inflation and all other variables behaving the way we hope they do. Anything that hasn't been planned can derail your entire plan and delay your financial freedom if you still have a shot at it. Well, I don't know for you, but for me, this is just too uncertain. To me, the only certainty is that it is not an attractive proposition.

Financial freedom methods based on real estate

The second major method is adopted by real estate investors, who typically don't trust Wall Street very much and prefer their perceived safety of "bricks and mortar" assets rather than paper assets. Real estate investors are primarily focused on cashflow they can get from rents. Appreciation is also important, of course, but cashflow will directly provide the income necessary for financial freedom. It looks perfect. However, there are a few problems here too. First, cash-flowing real estate properties generally have a minimum "entry ticket" that starts from at least high tens to a few hundreds of thousands of dollars. While this is no problem for many folks with available resources to buy properties outright, there are many people who cannot afford to buy them immediately: they will need to save and accumulate capital first before being able to afford them. This obviously takes time. The second problem is that unlike a paper asset, which Wall Street has made extremely easy and convenient for busy folks to invest in, "bricks and mortar" assets do require some work, especially initially. And this creates another problem: those who never invested in real estate before generally feel they don't even know how to get started. They feel they have no experience. They are afraid of "tenants & toilets" from horror stories they may have heard (normally blown out of proportion for dramatic effects). They feel they need proper investor education first, and they are right.

The good news about traditional methods, despite the downsides mentioned, is that they do work for some people, especially those on the higher end of the income spectrum. Millions of people around the world have achieved financial freedom one way or another. The problem is, again: at what cost? High income earners will undoubtedly have it easier. These folks will get there one way or another; the only difference is how fast. But what about the common person? Or young people starting out their careers? Shouldn't everyone else deserve a chance too? The goal of the AFFF is not to revolutionize, but to make important changes to existing methods creating an improved framework so that more people can also achieve financial freedom and faster. Those at the top can also benefit from the AFFF because it will accelerate their journeys too. As you will soon learn, the AFFF aims to both reduce the travel distance and increase velocity at the same time to speed up your journey to financial freedom.

The cow and milk analogy

I love analogies because they help us understand concepts. Take the following analogy, for example. Imagine you are a farmer raising cattle. If you survive by eating your cows, one day, there will probably not be a cow left alive and your herd is gone forever. But if you survive by drinking their milk instead, you will continually be able to do so because you will still have your herd intact, if not larger. This simple analogy explains the concepts of income and wealth. Milk is income. Cattle is wealth. When you withdraw 4% or whatever percentage annually from your portfolio of stocks and bonds, you are actually eating it away piece by piece. Your assumption (which to me is more like hope) is that the portfolio will grow by at least 4% every year to replace the dollars you withdrew. Well, in some years it will, but in some other years it won't. You know what happened to the stock market in 2022. It did not go up by 4%. In fact, the S&P 500 lost almost 20% in 2022. Hey, you just ate a bigger slice of your cow than you had expected that year! What about bonds? Bonds also lost in 2022. That's why I think that taking withdrawals from growth portfolios as income is a bad idea. I think we should always have a clear distinction of what is income and what is value appreciation in our minds. Using a growth or value appreciation asset to extract income from it will create problems and inefficiencies. Only income can efficiently offset expenses, not capital gains from growth or value appreciation.

Taking withdrawals from growth portfolios for income is generally a bad idea

Only income can efficiently offset expenses

Again, I'm not against any particular method. But when you compare them, differences stand out and become obvious. I will show you throughout the book why the AFFF is much more efficient than all these methods because it is far more comprehensive, smarter, and more ambitious:

- The AFFF will go beyond financial freedom, aiming to ensure financial security, retirement security, and legacy planning (by mitigating longevity risk).
- The AFFF will explore multiple assets to give you maximum thrust to your engines to complete your journey faster than single-asset type methods.
- The AFFF will explore leverage opportunities to boost your speed even faster.
- The AFFF will teach you money optimization techniques that will help you extract more bang from your buck.

The AFFF is not tied to any industry interest groups. It was designed having the end user in mind at the center. I am an end user myself. As you have just seen, the AFFF transcends industries and industry norms. All these things integrated in a method make it superior to others, in my view. If you are thinking, "Oh, great, but it must be hard to understand and to implement," bear with me. Give me a chance to explain it to you, show you how and why it works, and finally how you can implement this, with or without my help. It is actually very simple. But since you may have been brainwashed by traditional media for so long, it may take a while for new ideas to sink in. So, take your time, learn the new concepts, think about them, reflect, and I'm sure you will find the journey more than worthwhile.

CHAPTER 3

3. The Accelerated Financial Freedom Formula™: a simple but powerful idea

How can you accelerate financial freedom? I will explain how. Bear with me. First, imagine you are about to go on a trip. To shorten the travel time of a trip, any trip, there are only two ways:

- Increase your speed or
- Shorten the distance to your destination

Therefore, this is exactly the central idea behind the AFFF, which will do **both** things at the same time: increase speed AND shorten the travel distance.

To become financially free, you will need to buy assets that can generate the income you desire and cover all your living expenses (let's call this desired income your "**Target Income**"). But you need money to buy such income-generating assets in the first place, don't you? Perhaps you do have this money readily available, perhaps you don't. Most people don't. Thus, to get this money (let's call this amount of money your "**Target Capital**"), you will need to save money every month, invest it, and accumulate it with all your investment gains until you get the required Target Capital. Makes sense? Look at the diagram below.

Here's the analogy: It is just like climbing a staircase to get to Target Capital first, then using this money to buy income-generating assets to produce the Target Income you desire. The 4% Rule used in a traditional method to reach financial freedom works on this exact principle.

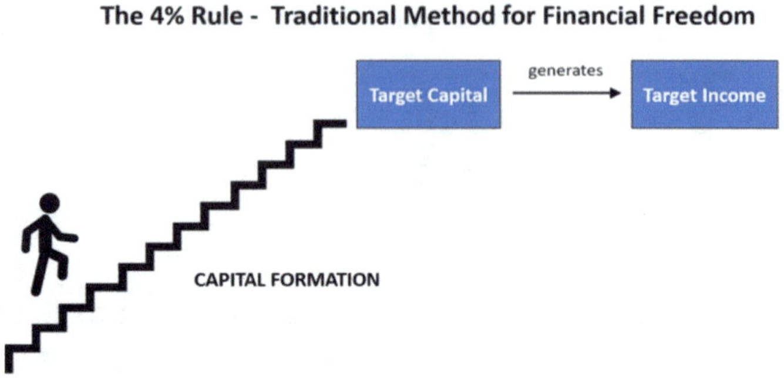

Very well. If you understood this simple concept, let's take one more step forward.

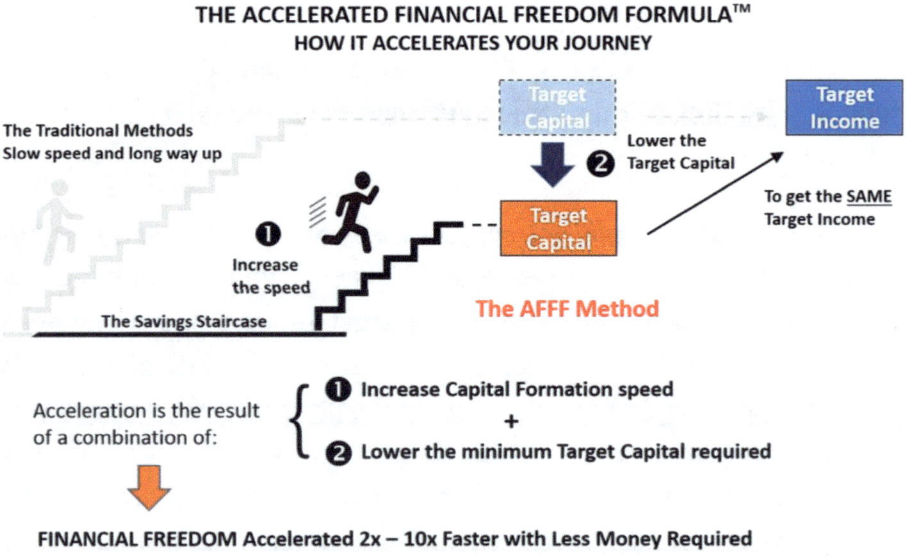

The AFFF strategy involves two stages – **Stage I** (climbing up the stairs or growing your capital) and **Stage II** (lowering the required Target Capital for the desired Target Income). Now the AFFF is ready to step in to accelerate this whole process. Ready?

The AFFF will accelerate the process by doing two things:

- ❶ Increasing the climbing speed AND
- ❷ Lowering the minimum Target Capital required

❶ Increasing the climbing speed to arrive at the top (Target Capital) faster is accomplished by employing the first and the second principles of the AFFF's four principles. This will be explained at length, later in the book. You will choose high appreciation assets. Read on!

❷ Lowering the Target Capital equals shortening the travel distance. If you shorten the travel distance (less steps to climb!), you will certainly reach the top (Target Capital) sooner, even if the speed has not changed. But note that the final destination in terms of your financial freedom income (the Target Income) remains the same even though the Target Capital was lowered. To accomplish this feat, we will employ the third principle of the AFFF.

This is just a brief introduction. The AFFF will be properly explained, and I also offer a step-by-step action plan (The Flightplan) for you to implement for your own journey to financial freedom. By increasing the travel speed and shortening the travel distance, you will naturally and undoubtedly arrive at the destination faster. This is the only possible outcome. By doing the same with your investments, the AFFF will invariably guide you to **reach your financial freedom faster with less money required**.

At this point, maybe you are impressed or maybe you are not (yet). So, let me make another statement that will shock you. The AFFF will take you **way beyond** financial freedom. According to the definition of financial freedom, this is when your new income through investments equals or exceeds your desired Target Income level. At this level, you may quit your job, if you so desire, because your investment income may fully replace the income you used to earn from your job. Most proponents of financial freedom will guide you up to this point. I call this important milestone **Basic Financial Freedom**. The AFFF is actually designed to take you further to what I call **Full Financial Freedom**, when your retirement is also secure after solving the longevity risk problem.

Are you incredulous?

If you are, I don't blame you. And you wouldn't be alone. In your shoes, I certainly would have doubted it if someone made such claims to me before. If I hadn't found the principles that made the AFFF viable, experienced the transformation in my own life and in the lives of others, I too would seriously doubt if it were even possible.

If you are incredulous, it's perfectly normal. I would only ask you a small favor. Try to put the skepticism aside for a moment while you read the rest of what I have to share with you. If, after learning the contents of this book, you aren't totally convinced and want to bring the skepticism back, it's okay. But I bet you will be pleasantly surprised, as I will prove my points to you, even mathematically!

I said I'm confident in the results of the AFFF because, besides myself, I have seen how so many people have achieved financial freedom with just parts of the AFFF. Many of them completed their journeys even without the full framework of the AFFF. They just took longer in their journeys to conquer financial freedom, but they did get there. The AFFF's goal is to speed up the entire journey and require less money to allow more people to reach this destination faster compared with traditional methods.

The AFFF is not a revolutionary secret formula created overnight out of a eureka moment. In fact, it was developed after numerous trials with as many failures and successes, which became a collection of lessons learned over a very long period of time. I would say this has taken half my lifetime so far. The key principles or pillars of the AFFF were not invented by me. The instruments or vehicles used to implement the AFFF are for the most part widely known in public. My contribution in formulating the AFFF was to join and arrange the various fragmented pieces into an integrated framework working more efficiently together for a clear purpose to speed up the journey to our intended destination. I added the "Accelerated" piece to the puzzle so we could achieve financial freedom multiple times faster than normal.

Another goal behind the development of AFFF was to make it easier for people to understand the principles and have a useful roadmap in their hands to confidently implement it step by step and reach their financial freedom and beyond. The AFFF is also intended to help people see why financial freedom is possible with solid proof that is mathematical because they may be confused. We are bombarded by all kinds of opinions from multiple sources, and often they are conflicting, which leads to confusion. Often, we really don't know what to believe anymore. For example, I was told by doctors and mainstream sources not to eat eggs because of fat and cholesterol, and I avoided them for decades. In recent years, I found that advice to be a huge mistake. Confusion leads to paralysis, and nothing ever gets done.

Before we dive into the details of the AFFF, you must be wondering how I came up with all this knowledge. I'm going to share with you my personal journey.

My own journey: who I am and how I came up with the AFFF

As you may have suspected, obstacles and adversities I faced in my career pushed me to search for the "secrets" of the rich, but especially the holy grail to break free from active income dependency. Born to a middle-class family of immigrants from Taiwan to Brazil, where I grew up and then immigrated again to the United States, I'm the second generation of migrants looking to settle somewhere to work hard and make a decent living. When my parents emigrated to Brazil in 1973, I was just 5 years old. My family experienced hardships. From them, I learned the value of honesty, respect, education, and hard work to achieve a decent standard of living.

I believe most good families teach these same basic principles to their children. Get the best education the family can afford, get a good paying and reputable job with benefits and a pension plan, and work hard to climb the corporate ladder. Start a family, stay away from debt, save for retirement, and invest in stocks and bonds. Work until retirement age, retire comfortably, and when your time has come, leave your children a legacy to help make their journey a little easier than your own. I'm sure you must have heard something similar from your parents too.

Like everyone else, I followed and lived by these principles. On the surface, it's a pretty simple plan. I also had dreams, goals to accomplish in life, and ambitions. These principles were time-proven and very common sense. What could possibly go wrong?

Set up for success: what could go wrong?

As it turned out, as I graduated from college onto the workforce, launching what became a 20-year career in finance. I shockingly realized these basic and widely endorsed principles wouldn't produce the results I expected. The real world is nothing like what I had idealized. It's ruthless. It's dark, cutthroat, deeply unjust, and definitely not made for idealists.

On paper, I was very well positioned for a flawless, successful career. In terms of education, I pursued my dream schools very hard early on and fought insane competition. I graduated from the best university in Brazil, Universidade de Sao Paulo (USP), in 1991, and the renowned MBA program at the Wharton School of the University of Pennsylvania in 2002. Distinguished alumni from my class at Wharton include Sundar Pichai, Google's Alphabet Inc. CEO, and Neel Kashkari, president of the Federal Reserve Bank of Minneapolis.

I also attended other programs to further improve my education. Later, while working during the day, I added a few night classes to my academic journey from the Master of Science for Mathematics in Finance program at the Courant Institute for Mathematical Sciences at New York University (NYU). Earlier, while still at Wharton, I also took a half-semester of courses as an exchange student at Insead Business in Fontainebleau, France.

In terms of competition for top jobs, I did pretty well. I worked for large and well-known international banks, such as Lloyds Bank, ABN Amro, Citigroup, BBVA, and Morgan Stanley, in New York, Hong Kong, and Sao Paulo. I had the opportunity to work at the forefront of derivatives trading based on currency, interest rates, and stock markets. I have experienced several severe financial crises since the early 1990's in volatile emerging markets, while responsible for hundreds of millions to a few billion dollars of my employer's and clients' money. I also had the opportunity to experience many functions in the trading floor as an analyst, trader, deal structurer, product developer, portfolio manager, and risk manager.

I had been enjoying a pretty successful and solid career, so you may be wondering what went wrong. In fact, I enjoyed every minute working in the trading floor with markets and clients. I also enjoyed all the challenges I faced, problems I had to solve, simple and complex, big and small. I always welcomed a good intellectual challenge. But under the surface, things were pretty ugly. The rug was pulled so many times from under me that I lost count. My inability and unwillingness to play office politics weren't going to take me very far. Not having powerful "protectors" also meant easy prey. Just being a good worker, a hard worker, and delivering solid results alone unfortunately wasn't sufficient to take me very far up the corporate ladder, I painfully realized. I don't know about you, but perhaps you can relate to my experience.

For over 20 years, I worked for 5 different banks and an energy trading company. There, I was so brutally bullied by a supervisor that I quit in less than 3 months. That was my worst experience ever in a workplace. My fellow colleagues witnessed everything because the plan was to embarrass me publicly in front of everybody. They even felt sorry for me. I still wonder why that person chose me as his target. I did my work well, treated everyone with respect, and wasn't by far the weakest performer in the team. There wasn't really a professional or any type of reason for the bullying. All I could think of was, perhaps, I was the only Ivy League graduate among people who weren't, including the offender himself, or maybe even my race might have played a role, as well. I never really knew. The fact of the matter is that I'm long past any anger or resentment. I brought up the example only to make a point that anyone can have a miserable life at work or even be suffering in silence. Not because of the work itself, which may be highly enjoyable, but because of people around you, especially those given power over you.

Corporate bullies are actually cowards because they only do what they do behind the safety of the belief that you won't ever risk your career hitting back.

Moving to a different company often helps initially; but over time, the managers who hired you will leave and the new supervisor usually sees you as a competitor and the toxic environment starts all over again. Have you ever encountered a similar situation or seen it happen for a colleague in your workplace? At one company, my hiring manager was ousted in a power struggle in less than 6 months from my hiring date. His opponent who took over control of the team believed I was my ex-boss' man. Actually, I wasn't, but he believed I was. Without a shred of evidence (because it wasn't true anyway), he blatantly discriminated against me, blocking me from career advancement opportunities even though I was delivering increasing profits for the firm with every passing year.

The last straw for me came after an interview with a top bulge bracket investment bank in Asia. I was by far the best candidate, and my unique combination of experiences positioned me first for the job, according to the recruiter. I will explain to you why that was true. In the early 2010's, the commodities market was booming, and China was hungry for raw materials like iron, copper, and other minerals Brazil had in abundance. This positive symbiosis pushed both Chinese and Brazilian economies to make up the so-called BRICS countries (Brazil, Russia, India, China, South Africa). The bank saw an opportunity to position itself in the middle of that booming commerce. They wanted to hire a trader who could speak both Portuguese and Chinese Mandarin. Well, not many people could, but I did. They also wanted someone who had experience with interest rates, currency, and stocks in both countries. Even fewer people would qualify for this requirement, but I still did. Such a combination was so rare that I was pretty much the only serious contender for the job. I also had U.S. markets experience. But still I wasn't given more than one interview. Of course, the real reason for the rejection won't ever be revealed, but I highly suspect it was the manager's unspoken fear of hiring a potential future competitor. The only thing he said was that I was "overqualified." Have you ever heard someone say that to you as an excuse to block your application for a job position? I bet you have or know someone who has heard.

To me, it became clear I needed to find a permanent solution. I really didn't want to live the rest of my life like that. If I could just replicate the same income I was making from my job at the bank from other sources that I could control, bingo! Since I wasn't a famed artist, entertainer, inventor, or even a writer to create royalty or patent-generated income, I couldn't initially see a way out. But I knew a lot about finance and markets! I must find a way to make it work from investments, I thought. However, it's easier said than done. After much seeking for the holy grail of financial freedom (or should I say the freedom provided by finance?), I was eventually able to free myself from what had nothing to do with the idealized corporate career I had anticipated.

Financial freedom, however, was for a very long time an alien concept to me. I believe it is still alien for most people, and that was the main motivation for launching the AFFF project. I want to share and disseminate to all corners of the world information for anyone who also wants to free themselves from the tyranny of the modern corporate power structure or for whatever other reason for wanting to become financially free (and fast!). Please do not lose hope.

Freedom is valuable, worth fighting for

I know many people love their jobs, their managers, and their colleagues. They are on track to promotion after promotion. I'm happy for them. I really am. I think they are lucky, and that should be cherished. In my case, I wasn't that fortunate. And believe me, I tried hard. I longed for financial freedom because I was tired of disgusting office politics, corporate power struggles, toxic environments, incompetent managers, and frustration after frustration. I'm sure many of you reading my personal story can relate after having experienced something similar and dream about leaving that toxic world behind. A simple test to determine how much you really love (or hate) your job is asking yourself how you feel on Sunday nights and Friday mornings. Take the test and don't lie to yourself.

If you feel miserable Sunday night and happy Friday morning, it is a clear sign your job is not bringing you the happiness and satisfaction you deserve.

Lack of motivation, frustration, stress, and even anger felt over a long period of time will gradually build and take a heavy toll on your mental and physical health. It lowers your immune system defenses, increases cortisol in the blood stream, and leads to chronic diseases. Prolonged exposure to a toxic work environment does lasting damage to people's mental and physical health and robs them of their joy to be productive members of society. Don't let this happen to you. Our lives and health are far more valuable than any compensation we get from an employer. If money (or the lack thereof) is what is holding you prisoner, you should seriously consider learning and immediately start working towards your financial freedom in an accelerated fashion to expand your choices.

Freedom is valuable and worth fighting for, always remember that. Don't be fooled by the apparent freedom we supposedly enjoy in society. Paraphrasing my favorite history teacher in high school, Mr. Jobson, "In the Middle Ages, people's conduct was blatantly compulsory. In modern life, it is covertly free." Remember: the relative freedom we enjoy today has been fought for and often paid for in blood.

But for financial freedom, fortunately, no blood is required. You need only the right knowledge, a time-tested strategy, and a relentless determination to succeed.

The system is all wrong: it really should not be like this

It really should not be like this. There is something very wrong with our modern society. Honest, hardworking people really should not be subjected to these kinds of injustices and feel miserable at work. Above all, they should not be chained to jobs they hate because they are just too afraid to quit and run out of money to support their families.

The sad reality is that people have different reasons to be tightly bound to a job they hate. But most of these reasons are centered around money in one way or the other. That's actually the good news because money problems do have solutions. They may be hard to find, but someone eventually will, like I did.

Ross' story

I'm certainly not alone. I heard a friend of mine (let's call him Ross, not his real name) complain about his job, his managers, his colleagues, and even his clients every time we spoke, over the course of almost a decade. Everything about his work environment seemed toxic. Ross, 54, daydreamed about his retirement, though it was still a good 11 years away. He said he felt miserable just by the thought of returning to the office every morning. Friday was his favorite day of the week and Sunday was his worst. “So why do you keep putting up with this and don’t find another job or just quit?” I asked.

On the financial side, Ross wasn’t in bad shape. After so many years of hard work, Ross did manage to save a substantial amount of money in his retirement accounts (401k, IRA, etc.) and even had some savings and stock investments on the side. He had no significant debts; his home was paid off and his young adult children had already gained their independence living elsewhere. In fact, Ross was doing significantly better than most Americans (see exhibit in the frame below). In theory, Ross shouldn’t have been that afraid of quitting his job. But when asked why not leave, his answer shocked me. He said he couldn’t do it because he needed the health insurance from the firm. If he had to pay health insurance privately, out-of-pocket, his savings wouldn’t be enough to sustain his intended lifestyle. Plus, there would be another problem: what if Ross outlived his life expectation? With modern advances in medicine, people are living longer than previous generations. Would his nest egg savings survive that long? That was his dilemma and drama. I suggested he start learning the principles of the AFFF to take the first steps towards his financial freedom. “Is it too late for me?” he asked. Nope. It’s never too late. But older folks will have less margin for error. It should not be delayed further because it takes time to build up assets. Financial freedom is a journey after all.

How America Saves 2022 – A Vanguard Report

According to the 2002 How America Saves report published by Vanguard, in 2021, the median American 401(k) balance is … $35,000! Thus, for the average man, this is most likely about all he/she had saved for retirement. The report also showed that about 40%, or two in every five folks, have less than $20,000. This is even more shocking, especially considering that since the same report published in 2012, it hasn't changed much in the last 10 years – remember the U.S. stock market (S&P 500) experienced the longest bull market on record, returning 325% during the same period. This doesn't even include the losses in the early months of 2022. A bull market is a market in which prices rise consistently.

Retirement savings do vary significantly by age and income. The average person in the survey is in their mid-40s. Older folks typically have more money saved, as expected. But not much better. The median person between the ages of 55 and 64 has a balance of around $90,000. In terms of income, the difference is even more pronounced. Those earning less than $50,000 annually save less than 7% of their income. Those earning $100,000 to $150,000 saved a little above 9%.

The findings of the Vanguard report are not only shocking, but also sad. It is not supposed to be like this. The reality is that it's very hard to save on low income, let alone seek and achieve financial freedom. Most people simply believe such a feat is impossible. And it may be true for many people. But with hope, the right strategy, and a little bit of luck, things may turn out well in the end.

Lack of proper financial education and brainwashing by mainstream sources

Have you ever wondered why most of us went to school but were never properly taught entrepreneurship and financial literacy? The education system was actually designed to produce workers for the manufacturing and services sectors. In college, you immerse yourself in your chosen field, and unless it's business or finance, you won't ever learn entrepreneurship, finance, and investments. Isn't that true? Then, later in life, you wonder why you never thought about starting your own business and why you know so little about managing your own finances or making investment decisions. If you feel down about this, you should know it's not your fault. The education system was designed this way on purpose.

Notwithstanding the first blow, here comes the second: brainwashing by the official mainstream sources taught us how to make investments. What have you learned? Live debt-free, invest in mutual funds, buy CD's (Certificates of Deposit)? Save for retirement by placing all your savings in qualified plans (e.g., 401k, IRA, etc.) because of the tax-deferred "advantage"? The entire system was designed to favor the system itself. It wasn't designed with you at the center, you can be sure of that.

What about financial freedom? I admit I had no clue until much later in my life. Since childhood, most of us in middle-class families have been taught and made to believe (by family, teachers, media, etc.) that the only way to achieve financial freedom was by working hard and accumulating enough wealth. That's the principle of accumulation. The evidence can be seen everywhere. People work their entire lives to save, live debt-free, and invest their hard-earned savings in financial instruments (stocks, bonds, etc.), real estate, and retirement accounts. They do exactly what they were taught. Wall Street created a plethora of convenient ways, heavily advertised to help us do that. But think about it: if this is the ultimate solution, why are most people still not financially free and struggle every day? Why do they still depend on a regular paycheck and employer benefits to make ends meet? Why the Vanguard Report is so gloomy? The answer is not that the products they created aren't good. They are. But how you deal with them needs to be improved. We need better methods.

How I saw the light and structured the AFFF

By now, you know a little about me, my personal journey, my struggles, and what motivated me to search for the holy grail of personal finance: financial freedom.

Before we dive into the core of the AFFF to explain all about it, I think it's also important that you know how I first learned about financial freedom and how I was able to assemble the essential puzzle pieces of the AFFF. Of course, it did not fall from the sky into my lap on a beautiful summer day. Nor did it come to me through divine inspiration and, voilà, I decided to find out all about it. In fact, it took me years of learning, trial and error attempts, many victories, many setbacks, and I can certainly say that it is still a never-ending, continuous process of learning, improvement, and refinement. But after a long period of testing, analyzing results, learning from mistakes, and amassing knowledge in multiple markets or asset classes, I am confident that the core principles and pillars of AFFF are solid. They work and can achieve tangible, real results.

What do you gain by learning from me? Besides saving you from sweat, tears, and dead ends, it will save you – **T I M E** – the most precious asset we all are born with, but we often neglect. Every one of us, whether you're Warren Buffett or Jimmy Buffett, are born with a finite number of years, days, and hours to live on this Earth. Therefore, time is much more valuable than money. By learning the AFFF to guide and implement your own journey, you will save years of trials and mistakes someone else (me) has already made before you. This *per se* should be considered an accelerator for your financial freedom!

Markets are fragmented

Think about it: how is the investment world in our society organized? It's highly fragmented, and I will explain how and why. For instance, say you are a real estate investor. Who can help you buy properties? Real estate agents. They are regulated by each state's real estate board. What if you want to invest in stocks, who can help you then? Stock brokers. These folks are regulated by completely different regulators, which in this case are the national and state securities authorities. Real estate professionals think and breathe real estate. Some agents don't discuss investments because they serve people looking for homes to move into. Conversely, financial professionals rarely want to discuss real estate investing and always turn the discussion away from it because that is not their specialty. Even the language each camp uses and their educational credentials are worlds apart.

See where I'm going? You, as an investor, want to have as many options available as possible so you can explore the best of both worlds. Given the moment's economic conditions and the respective markets, you need to have as many weapons in your investment arsenal as possible. But the entire investment framework isn't designed with you, the investor, in mind. It's designed for the "sell side" to facilitate sale of real estate or financial assets to you, but it was not designed for you on the "buy side." For example, have you ever mentioned you wished to invest in real estate to a financial advisor? What has been his/her reaction? Have they ever embraced the idea? Probably not. It's not their forte, and financial advisors won't get paid a commission if you invest in real estate. So, they will always try to steer you away from the idea. If you insist, they may offer you a real estate ETF (Exchange-Traded Fund) or an REIT (Real Estate Investment Trust), instead. These alternatives aren't really the best ways to invest in real estate, in my opinion. But it's not their fault and they certainly aren't bad people. But the point I want you to understand is that the investment landscape is very fragmented and the industry is built to favor the industry itself, not you and me.

Here's a very important point: we should not let this fragmentation limit our ability to explore investment opportunities. That's exactly one of the core principles of the AFFF: the ability to access the most markets possible and the ability to switch between asset types and markets at the right time. Don't let the system limit your choices. This is the first key to accelerating a journey to financial freedom!

My first breakthrough

And that was my first breakthrough in my journey to financial freedom: tear down walls separating industries and fields in which I could be investing. I am a finance guy, formed from a business school and decades of experience in the financial services industry. I lived and breathed Wall Street every day for 20 years. I didn't know much (or anything) about real estate investments. A few years after the financial crisis of 2008, which preceded the bottoming out of the U.S. real estate market in 2010, I set my sights on real estate seriously for the first time. [Side note: I realized early on from data that some real estate markets in the country more or less lagged the stock market by a few years – and yes, I'm a data nerd]. As a trader who was always timing the markets to make profits and avoid losses, I thought I could use this realization to profit from the housing market as well. From 2008 to 2010, the stock market was already recovering and trending up, while the real estate market was still losing ground. See the S&P 500 index and Case-Schiller Home Price Index in the chart below.

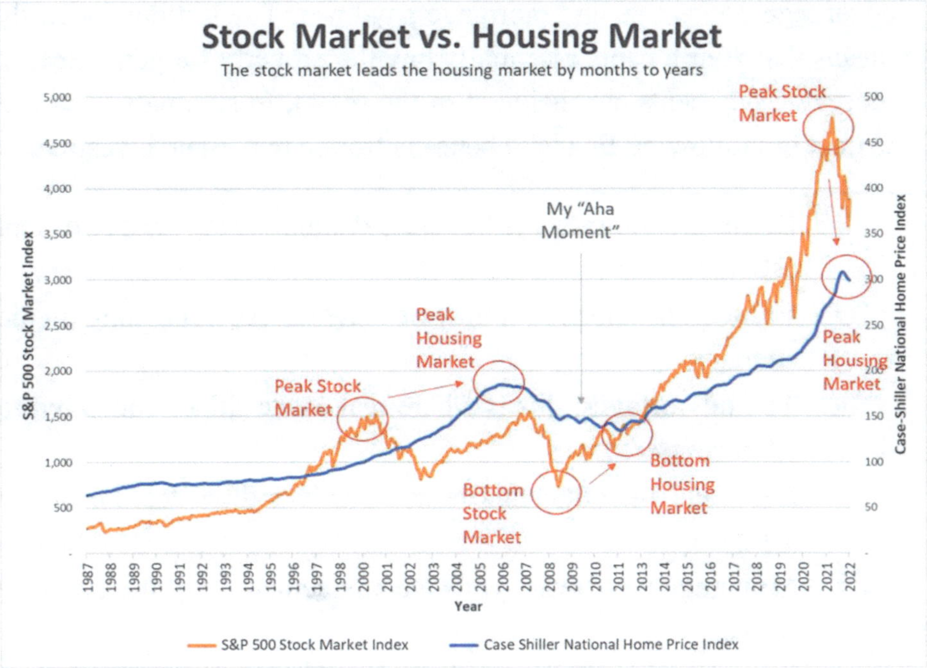

This was my aha moment. The stock market cycle could be an early indicator about the real estate market cycle. This is when I decided to learn more about this asset class and started planning my first investment around 2010, near the bottom of the real estate market.

I soon realized that real estate is the perfect asset type to produce the income for financial freedom. For those of us in the finance industry, real estate can be thought of an instrument like a dividend-paying stock, in a way. But the rental yield from real estate can far exceed tiny stock dividend yields. Real estate prices can also appreciate like stocks, though at a much slower pace and without the volatility. That's why I got attracted to real estate in the first place: income plus appreciation potential.

However, at that moment, I was not really versed in real estate investing like I am today. Nevertheless, I started to learn fast and quickly found out about other equally attractive benefits: tax advantages, leverage, and mortgage paydown. The last one basically means that your tenants essentially buy the property for you (because mortgage payments are included in the rents). In summary, you can extract the following financial benefits from a real estate investment:

- **Rental income**: this is the main distinguishing feature of real estate
- **Value appreciation**: it may be slow or fast, depending on the strategy
- **Tax advantages**: this is where real estate shines compared to all other asset types
- **Leverage benefits**: this is another incredible feature of the asset class
- **Mortgage paydown:** your tenants actually buy the property for you

How do you determine the rental yield (return from rents) on a real estate investment? –

Initially, like many beginners, I also had no clue how I could calculate the rental return of a real estate investment, let alone judge whether it was a good deal or not. Soon, I figured out that it was actually quite simple, not complicated at all. We use a projected income statement called "pro-forma" just as the example in the image below. You may download the Excel sheet I used from my author website. You project rents and expenses, and based on the price (or value) of the property, you estimate the yield return. I'm showing two pro-formas for the same property. The one on the left is an all-cash acquisition, without leverage (or bank loan). You are buying the property with your own resources. The pro-forma on the right is a leveraged acquisition where a bank loan will cover 80% of the property's value. Your out-of-pocket cost to acquire the property is just 20% of its value, plus closing costs.

Real Estate Investment Pro-forma
(No leverage simple model)

Home price	225,000	
Closing costs	3,375	1.5%
Investment amount	**228,375**	
Estimated Income Statement (annual figures)		
Gross rents	30,000	
(+) Other income	1,500	
(-) Management fee	(1,800)	6%
(-) Taxes	(4,500)	
(-) Insurance	(3,500)	
(-) Landlord paid bills	(1,440)	
(-) Repairs/maintenance	(900)	3%
(-) Vacancy & losses	(1,200)	4%
Total Expenses	(13,340)	
Net Income/loss	**18,160**	
Cap Rate	**8.0%**	
Cash on Cash Return	**8.0%**	

Real Estate Investment Pro-forma
(Leveraged simple model)

Home price	225,000	
Loan-to-Value (LTV)	80%	
Loan tenor	30	years
Loan interest rate	4.50%	
Loan amount	180,000	
Investor down-payment	45,000	
Closing costs	3,375	1.5%
Loan closing costs	3,375	1.5%
Investment amount	**51,750**	
Estimated Income Statement (annual figures)		
Gross rents	30,000	
(+) Other income	1,500	
(-) Management fee	(1,800)	6%
(-) Taxes	(4,500)	
(-) Insurance	(3,500)	
(-) Landlord paid bills	(1,440)	
(-) Repairs/maintenance	(900)	3%
(-) Vacancy & losses	(1,200)	4%
(-) Mortgage payment	(10,944)	
Total Expenses	(24,284)	
Net Income/loss	**7,216**	
Cap Rate	**8.0%**	
Cash on Cash Return	**13.9%**	

The return on investment (ROI) in real estate for all-cash acquired properties is called the "**cap rate.**" The ROI in real estate for leveraged properties is called the "**cash-on-cash return.**" Therefore, if you are buying a property without a loan, the cash-on-cash return will be equal to the cap rate. But in a leveraged property, cash-on-cash return must be greater than the cap rate for leverage to make sense. In other words, you should only seek leverage if the cap rate is greater than the cost of borrowing. In the example above, the loan interest rate is less than the cap rate, and closing costs aren't too high; thus, the cash-on-cash return is higher than the cap rate. Therefore, it is a good deal if you can get it financed.

How to calculate the amount of property needed to generate the income I want - Can I do the reverse, I mean given the income amount I want to target, say $100,000 a year, find out how much property I should buy to generate that income for me? The answer is yes. Provided that you have properties in mind, and you know their cap rates, you just do the calculation in reverse. For example, in the no leverage case, you can see that this property delivers $18,160 for a $225,000 property, or $0.08 for each $1.00 of property (it's the cap rate!). Therefore, if you want $100,000 net income, just divide it by 0.08, and you will get roughly $1.2 million. But if you take the leveraged case, this property delivers $7,216 for $51,750 down-payment, or $0.14 for each $1.00 of your investment (it's the cash-on-cash return!). Therefore, if you want $100,000 net income, just divide it by 0.14, and you will get roughly $717,000. So, this is the math involved. It is not complicated; it just takes some practice. You can download the pro-forma in Excel and put in your own numbers. But hey, how am I supposed to buy a $717,000 property if it is selling for $225,000? Well, you can find similar other ones to buy so that the total investment is close to $717,000. You can seek 8% or higher cap rate properties. It doesn't need to be a single property. The income they produce should add up to your Target Income.

For my first steps towards financial freedom, I saw real estate as the starting building block because of the income it could produce for me passively. Did I say passively? Well, yes, but not in the sense I had believed, which I guess is also probably what you must be thinking. Some people say real estate investing is passive; some say it's not. The answer is both yes and no. I will elaborate more later on.

Is real estate the answer?

Some in the mainstream sources recommend retirees live off dividends from stocks. But the average dividend yield is only about 3%. Someone looking to replace an income of $80,000 would need to invest $2.7 million. Attractive? How about an income of $100,000? You would need a portfolio worth $3.4 million to produce an annual income of $100,000 at 3%. Would it be feasible and attractive to you? How long would you have to save to accumulate $3.4 million?

Some experts would argue that you could aim for high dividend-paying stocks, which could go as high as 8%, the so called "Dividend Aristocrats." A company is considered a dividend aristocrat if it has raised its dividends consistently for at least the past 25 years. I see dividend-paying stocks as another weapon in the arsenal, with its pros and cons like any other weapon. Stocks are highly risky investments, and the timing of buying and selling will be crucial to determine your final result. Dividends of common stocks are paid at the discretion of the company's management. There's no guarantee a company paying a high dividend yield today will continue to do it in the future.

Therefore, for me in the finance industry, I wasn't seeing any obvious type of investment which would ideally offer me:

a) Stable cashflow: monthly income
b) High yield of annual return
c) Low taxes, fees, etc.
d) Low risk
e) Liquidity (access to or ability to convert to cash quickly when needed)
f) Passive or low demand for my time

From the income perspective, let's compare real estate to stocks with dividends and bonds in each of the attributes above:

a) **Winner: Real estate -** Real estate may have stable cashflow with long-term contracts and guarantees. Stock dividend yields may be stable, but yields are too low in comparison. Rental income from real estate is perfect for financial freedom purposes.

b) **Winner: Tie -** Real estate usually has higher yields if you choose investments right, but stocks typically have faster value appreciation potential.

c) **Winner: Real estate -** Real estate is very tax-advantaged compared to almost all other kinds of investments. Stocks and bonds are also taxed at low rates, but tax advantages of real estate are too overwhelming.

d) **Winner: Real estate -** Real estate values don't have the high volatility of financial markets. However, real estate investments may have varying degrees of risk, and they may cause you losses too.

e) **Winner: Stocks and Bonds** – Stocks and bonds are extremely liquid. The most traded ones can be bought and sold instantly. Real estate clearly wasn't designed for liquidity. However, there are locations and situations where you can sell a property in less than 15 days, but it's not the norm.

f) **Winner: Stocks and Bonds** – Generally, if you're not a day trader, watching stock prices and charts all day long, investing in financial assets won't take much of your time. Even if you track your financial investments daily (highly recommended!), you may do it in just a few minutes per day. Real estate will demand more time from you. But if you create the right structure and delegate operations, you can minimize your time involvement significantly.

For the reasons above, real estate rose to the top of my investor mind. But until the 2008 financial crisis, I knew next to nothing about real estate investing. Honestly, by that time, the only memory I had from real estate investing was a failed one.

Real estate investing looks easy. Can it fail?

Earlier, in my childhood, my parents had purchased a house located about 10 miles from our home in Suzano, Brazil. It was a newly built house in a planned community. It was beautiful, at least much prettier than our own house where we lived. My parents thought it was a good investment. They soon found their first tenant. In the next few years, the house was rented by several different tenants. My parents experienced some delinquencies but not very serious until they had to evict the last tenant, who tricked his way to living rent-free for over a year. By then, my parents had had enough. Once the defaulting tenant was finally locked out and the house was repossessed, my parents got the final blow: the house was literally destroyed, utilities unpaid, and neighbors angry. The house was minimally fixed and sold for half the original price my parents had paid. In the end, what was supposed to be a good investment turned out to be a horrible one. My parents had not only lost money and time, but a dream! Their dream of financial freedom was unceremoniously ended right there, never to be attempted again. This unfortunate episode left a profound mark on me and was almost like a trauma for the entire family. In my mind, real estate was not an investment option, never to be attempted again. As I learned, it's riddled with landmines!

Then a long time passed after that childhood experience. Fast forward to year 2010, as I was staring at the screen of the computer on my trading desk thinking about the chart above (S&P 500 vs. Case-Shiller home price index from 2008-2010). On a quiet afternoon after the busy trading hours, I started to think about real estate again. It really looked like a good moment to buy real estate, but first, I had to overcome that traumatic memory of failure. After all, we know of so many successful real estate investors out there; thus, I started thinking, why wouldn't I succeed as well? After studying successful investors and doing more research, I finally convinced myself that what happened to my parents should not prevent me from seeking success. Often, we are too easily disheartened by earlier failures. The right attitude should not be that of retreat. If it's a traumatic experience, we may need to take a break, yes, we may need time to heal, but then regroup and return to the battlefield. A battle setback shouldn't mean the war was lost! We should accept that life is just like a baby learning to take their very first steps. They will invariably fall and fall often. Should they give up walking for the rest of their lives because of earlier failures? Absolutely not! So why should we? The right attitude is to take the time to meticulously analyze and understand what went wrong, why, and how each of the mistakes could be avoided or prevented from ever happening again. Here, I share with you what I handwrote in my notes when I decided to return to the battlefield:

a) My parents rushed to buy the property without an investment plan. Most people do the same, which is amateurish. Investments must be run like you run a business. You must know beforehand when you will exit the investment (your investment horizon), under what conditions, and have clear investment objectives.
b) My parents had not done a proper analysis of the market, demographics, and never understood the friendliness of local tenancy laws for landlords.
c) My parents managed the property themselves at a distance, which is to say, they barely knew what was really going on inside the property. Was the property well kept? Utilities paid? Any violations on the property?

d) My parents treated the tenants with too much of a personal friendliness and too casually. Yes, you should treat them well and with respect, but it's primarily a commercial relationship, not a friendship. Everything should be in writing, no verbal agreements.

e) Any late payments must be immediately followed up. Late fees must be charged. Eviction must be enforced for non-payment of rents.

f) Rent agreements must be in writing, and every clause must be enforced, no exceptions.

g) If unable to manage the property yourself, vet a good property manager and make sure he/she fulfills their duties properly.

h) My parents failed to properly screen each tenant. Their rental histories should have been properly scrutinized with production of verifiable proof of income.

i) Deferred maintenance destroys property value over time and problems compound. At least an annual inspection should be done; no exceptions. If the tenant caused damages, he/she must pay for the repairs.

j) Always keep an eye on property values in the neighborhood. If significant changes that can negatively impact your investment happen, you may need to exit early.

My lessons learned… I hope they will be helpful to you too. In the Real Estate Module (information on how to download the contents in Chapter 11), I will address these issues in much more detail.

My becoming a professional real estate investor

This simple short list gave me the confidence I needed to get back in the game. I was basically learning from earlier mistakes. I was also doing something extremely important: investing like a professional.

As it turned out, this instantly helped me stand out from all the amateurish weekend investors. I never saw real estate investing as a passive activity. I was very much active because I really wanted to learn everything I could. Over time, I learned so much that I developed a quick method to find, screen, locate, evaluate, negotiate, invest, manage, and exit investment properties profitably. I even organized group investments with other investors to buy small multifamily properties in a process called Real Estate Deal Syndication. I did this professionally after I retired from my corporate career in 2012, and I was even paid to run the syndication with a portfolio of over 60 rental units.

So now I have added 10 years of real estate investing experience to my 20-year experience with financial markets! All it did for me was to enlarge the number of tools in my investor toolbox. Besides stocks, bonds, currencies, gold, and derivatives, now I had learned how to invest in real estate like a professional. My arsenal just got a lot more powerful with the latest addition to my journey and quest for financial freedom.

However, one last piece that came later to the puzzle blew my mind away. I called this OPM/I (Other People's Money from internal sources). With it, AFFF became whole, and the method was born. Now that you have learned the whole story of my journey, the rest of the book will explain everything to you in detail, the entire formula.

Real estate is powerful but not enough for the acceleration I wanted

Many people are raised with a deep distrust of bankers and Wall Street. Some of that is because they have been hurt before (lost money), while others simply have a hard time understanding financial instruments. These folks place their trust entirely on the bricks and mortar of real estate. But would real estate, as powerful as it is, be sufficient to achieve financial freedom? The answer is yes, because millions of people around the world in the past and present were able to achieve financial freedom with real estate investments alone. However, there are drawbacks too. The entry ticket is high and not everyone can afford to buy a property right off the bat; they would need to save and build up at least the minimum capital and credit, first. So, if someone wants to seriously speed up their financial freedom, he/she must look beyond real estate and take advantage of the entire spectrum of instruments available, including financial instruments like stocks and bonds. As I will show later in the book that financial instruments will help accelerate your journey to financial freedom and can build up your wealth faster.

Here's a perfect analogy. You can think of this as going to war with not a single weapon but all the weapons you can carry to the battlefield. Only with a complete arsenal of multiple types of weapons can you choose which weapon to deploy in response to each battlefield circumstance you may encounter. You want to give yourself options and the best chance at winning. Likewise, you should also launch your journey to financial freedom with the broadest arsenal you can assemble, including real estate, financial assets, and more, if possible. This is actually one of the key principles of the AFFF: a multi-asset approach will always trump a single-asset approach. And your best reward: it will help accelerate your journey to financial freedom, as I will demonstrate for you in this book.

Why I'm sharing the AFFF with the world

You may be wondering why I'm sharing the results of a lifetime of learning with the world. If it's so good as I'm claiming, why not just keep this all to myself? If that is what you are thinking, I get you, but the reasons are very simple.

First of all, the AFFF is not a goldmine where the more you mine, the richer you will become. I mean, this is not a finite resource that I must keep a secret from everyone else. Rather, the AFFF is an improved method to reach financial freedom. Everyone can achieve his/her own financial freedom independently, and this won't have any effect on anyone else. Perhaps it will attract envy from others seeing you succeed, though! You only need to reach financial freedom once, especially what I call Full Financial Freedom. If other people are also reaching theirs by using it, great! Their successes won't affect you or me or make us any less productive. It will only make me happy and give me a greater sense of fulfillment seeing others succeed with my method. So, there is really no reason to keep it a secret. If it works, I believe more people should know about it. In fact, it would be a sacrilege to be selfish and not share with the world. The more people joining me in achieving financial freedom in their lifetimes, the more this movement will resemble a freedom revolution. I never thought of myself as a revolutionary of any kind, and I don't intend to be one. But I think everyone should benefit from knowledge that can potentially change their lives.

In fact, for a very long time, I never really thought about organizing and putting together all the principles and key pillars of AFFF I have learned over the years in the battlefield into a method or a replicable, step-by-step formula for others to follow. I never thought I would author a book and create video content about this, either. Since 2015, I have helped many investors by sharing knowledge through public speaking events, private consulting, and by organizing group investment in syndicated real estate deals. I also helped many people structure insurance deals. And the focus has never been financial freedom. It has simply been maximizing returns by investing in real estate and the stock markets through the S&P 500 ETFs. I have also been writing a blog with my commentary on the U.S. stock market. You can find it here, if interested:

- Medium Blog: https://engineering-finance.medium.com

As you can see, I have been creating and sharing content for a few years now, and I love doing it. I decided to use a language most people, especially non-finance people, could understand. I strive to avoid jargon and stick to one idea at a time to avoid confusion and unnecessary complications. Some experts write long newsletters with more sophisticated analysis (and they charge a subscription fee). But in my case, I decided to write short, daily posts for non-finance folks that can be read in 2-3 minutes with ease and not charge anything. If I can help one person a day with one quick drop of wisdom, I feel happy already. If such little bit of information could have saved money for someone, or earned him/her a slightly better ROI, or perhaps even transformed their life in some way, I feel that my little effort was well worth it.

I don’t do this out of pure altruism. I have actually learned from so many great teachers and mentors in life to take me to where I am today. It’s just the right thing to do to pass the knowledge forward.

The idea about collecting all the knowledge and experience to develop it into a multi-asset financial freedom acceleration formula came to me quite late in my life, actually during the 2020 pandemic. At that time, I was selling most of the real estate investments that my investors and I had held since 2015 and 2016. It was not only because the market was peaking and I believed the end of the market cycle was approaching, but also because we had planned to exit in 5 to 7 years since starting those investments. With more free time and locked down by the pandemic in full force, I started thinking about how I could help more people in a meaningful way. I started asking what makes people wake up every day and gives them something to look forward to. What did they want to achieve in life? How could my life experience help someone else? Every morning, thousands of people commute to New York Penn Station, rushing to work. What would be their real final destination?

Financial freedom has been much sought but rarely found. This has been an elusive destination for some and an impossible destination for many. Will I be able to help everyone? I don't think so, unfortunately. But even if I can help one person, it's worth the effort. Have you ever heard the "Starfish story"? Here you go: "*A man spotted a girl throwing beached starfish back into the ocean. He said, 'Do you not realize that there are miles of beach and starfish all along it? You cannot possibly make a difference.' The girl listened, then bent down to pick up another starfish and threw it into the ocean. She said, 'It made a difference for that one.*'"

Maybe this will be my legacy to the world, so even if only one person in the whole world used my method and achieved real results with it, I'm already happy.

CHAPTER 4

4. The Accelerated Financial Freedom Formula™ (AFFF)

Let me now introduce to you the AFFF by first laying out its 4 main principles with a brief explanation and their respective analogies for easier comprehension. I will discuss them in greater detail extensively in the rest of the book.

Four Principles of the Accelerated Financial Freedom Formula™

1. **Multi-asset type approach** – it's based on the idea that you shouldn't go to the battlefield with a single weapon or travel to Mars with a single rocket engine. Rather, you should be armed with multiple weapons or travel to Mars with several rocket engines and boosters.

   In the AFFF, you should deploy a combination of multiple types of investments, including income production assets (e.g., real estate, etc.) and capital formation assets (e.g., stocks, etc.), instead of focusing on any single one.

2. **Timing investments to the context (economy & market cycles)** – the idea is very simple: know WHEN to deploy which weapon or fire which engine given the external conditions (which you don't control) for maximum performance and results.

In the AFFF, we must always respect the asset's market cycles and economic conditions. This principle comes naturally with the first principle because when you employ multiple assets, you must know when to use which one. In contrast, since most traditional methods are single-asset type focused (usually financial assets only or real estate only), they will never have this principle.

3. **Borrowing the strength of a greater force: leverage with OPM** – it's based on the idea that you should not rely on your own financial strength alone. Whenever possible, borrow the strength of a greater force. It's similar to adding booster rockets for maximum thrust and speed.

   In the AFFF, you can leverage your investments with OPM (Other People's Money) by borrowing the financial strength of a banking institution, an insurance company, or another entity that is more financially powerful than yourself, instead of relying solely on your own financial strength and resources.

4. **Money booster (optimizing the use of money)** – You want financial freedom, and some of you are saving money aggressively, making sacrifices for it, but do you know how money really works? Many people know the concept of compound earnings, but have you been taking full advantage of its power? Or have you been continually sabotaging it, cutting off growth too early? What about lost opportunity costs you might not even be aware of related to choosing inferior or wrong investments? What about money sitting idle, not working for you? How about wealth eroded by taxes, interests, and inflation? Is money escaping between your fingers without you even being aware? How many years were wasted by not

building assets for your financial freedom? Or by choosing bad assets? Wasting time and wasting money are synonymous: both delay your financial freedom! Lost opportunity cost and invisible money leaks are real and are happening to all of us, but the AFFF offers a solution to reduce these problems (see Chapter 9).

The secret of the AFFF is based on the strategic use and arrangement over time of these 4 principles. Under the AFFF framework, you will be strategically and selectively using the best investment instruments from the full spectrum of asset classes given the external economic environment to maximize acceleration towards your financial freedom. The key here is the root word ***strategy***. The AFFF is designed to educate and train people not only to create their own unique and personalized strategies based on their own life circumstances and goals, but also to base them on the prevailing economic conditions at large, which they don't control.

Understanding the Accelerated Financial Freedom Formula TM

Now that you understand the 4 principles of the AFFF, let's discuss the main idea that powers this concept I introduced to you early on in the book: How do you speed up a journey traveling from point A to point B? We have learned from physics 101 that there are only two possible ways:

Increase your speed or

shorten the travel distance

The Accelerated Financial Freedom Formula™ aims to do **both** for your financial freedom.

How? Remember this diagram previously introduced in Chapter 3:

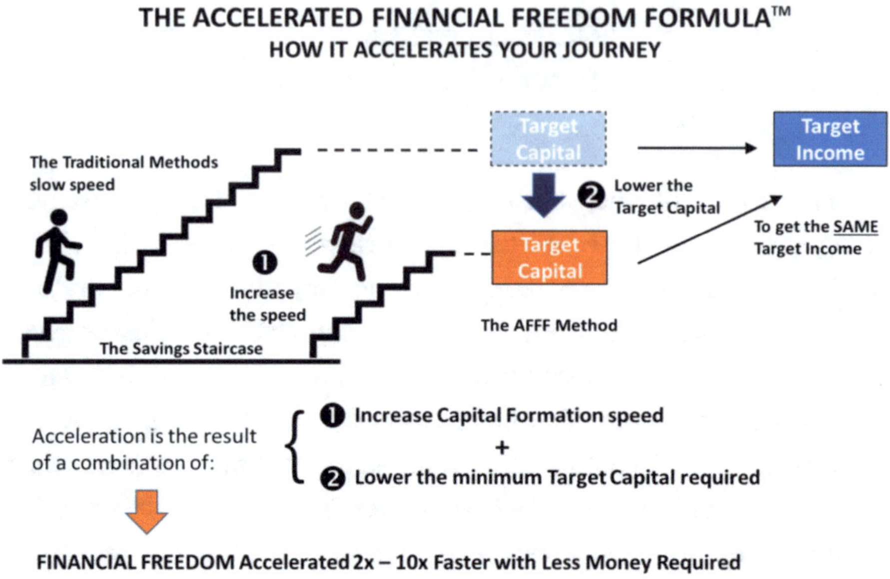

In Chapter 3, when I first introduced this diagram and explained that the AFFF is a two-stage process – ❶ **Stage I** (climbing up the stairs or growing your capital assets) and ❷ **Stage II** (buying income-generating assets with leverage to reduce money required) – I said that Stage I is powered by the first and second principles of the AFFF and that Stage II is powered by the third principle of the AFFF. But I did not explain how. Now that the four principles have been introduced and understood, let's discuss how Stages I and II can be accomplished.

In a nutshell, each stage has distinct goals and is implemented with different types of assets for maximum performance. The table below gives you an overview:

	Stage I: Capital Formation	**Stage II: Income Generation**
Objective	Build up capital	Generate income for you
Target to reach	Target Capital	Target Income
Type of asset	Growth assets	Income producing assets
Example of assets	Stocks, S&P 500, Outperform*, etc.	Real estate, Autorun Small Biz*
How to accelerate	High growth appreciation	High yield income cashflow
Use of leverage	Only if managing risk properly	Encouraged: OPM/E and OPM/I
Purpose of leverage	Accelerate growth speed	Reduce required Target Capital

* Explained later in the book

As you can see, Stages I and II serve very different purposes. Stage I's goal is growth because you want to build up capital faster (just like climbing the stairs faster) to get to the required Target Capital. Stage II's goal is to generate income for your financial freedom. Notice that traditional methods don't have this separation of the process into two stages. Traditional methods mix up capital buildup with income because they use only one single asset. Instead, the AFFF uses multiple assets; it strategically suggests growth assets to build up capital fast in Stage I and high yield income producing assets to pay you the most income in Stage II.

Here you can already see the first clue why the AFFF has to be more efficient than traditional methods by separating the process into two distinct stages – grow capital first and then generate income – so that you can maximize efficiency of the entire process.

Of course, if you are blessed to already have enough savings to make up the Target Capital for Stage II, you may not even need Stage I. But this isn't the case for most people, who will need Stage I to grow their life savings [fast] first.

Notice that we are applying the first two principles of the AFFF here already: multiple assets and choosing them strategically to maximize the acceleration of the entire process.

Next, let's apply the third principle of the AFFF, and that is the use of leverage (OPM: Other People's Money). In Stage II, leverage will reduce the required Target Capital. This happens because by borrowing capital from others (a bank, an insurance company, etc.), you don't need as much money from your own savings to buy Stage II assets! You are essentially reducing the required Target Capital that needs to come from Stage I. Therefore, notice that while Stage I will make you move faster towards your goal, Stage II will shorten the distance you need to travel (less stairs to climb!).

Got the idea? The only principle that I'm not going to illustrate here is the last of the four AFFF principles - Money Boosters (Optimize use of money). It's not easy to simulate it and it will be vastly different for everyone, but it is very powerful to accelerate your journey to financial freedom, as you will find out.

A numerical example to clarify the idea even more

I know that concepts may become confusing if they are novel and it's the first time someone is introduced to them. But a numerical example will do wonders. Let's compare the AFFF with the 4% Rule that is very popular, to which you may be more familiar, so you can see the differences more clearly.

Imagine a hypothetical person who has exactly the same financial situation as an **average** American. According to recent data, this person would have the following financial profile:

- **Annual income from work**: **$71,000** (Real median household income was $70,784 in 2021 according to the Census Bureau).
- **Available savings**: **$62,000** (Average amount of personal savings in 2022 came in at $62,000 according to the Northwestern Mutual Planning and Progress Survey 2022).
- **Savings rate**: **7%** (The average American typically saves between 6% and 8% of their monthly income according to First Republic Bank, 2022).

As you can see, I picked as an example someone who could be **a typical, average American, not rich and not poor, just average.** Financial advisors recommend that people should save 20% of their income but, unfortunately, this is easier said than done. So, let's not deceive ourselves with an idealized but unreal world and stick to reality. The reality is that people are saving less and less in the past few years. Let's take 7%, the midpoint between 6% and 8%. I know that FIRE followers, on the other hand, engage in a super-aggressive savings regime. While their intentions are very noble and I do admire their determination and resilience, I think they may ease up a little if they follow the AFFF method instead. I will show why in a moment, below.

Target Income - Let's say that this person wants a passive annual income of **$100,000**, which is 40% above his/her current income, to feel very secure about financial freedom. Certainly, with such a margin, this income will be enough to cover 100% of their current lifestyle expenses, but probably also future lifestyle expenses (our lifestyle changes over time, of course).

Let's first see how long this person would take to reach financial freedom with the traditional 4% Rule method. Then we will compare it with the AFFF so you can clearly see the difference.

Achieving financial freedom through a Traditional Method (The 4% Rule)

Applying the 4% Rule for this person to be able to withdraw $100,000 per year (or $8,333 per month) as income, they must aim to build a portfolio worth at least $2.5 million. To calculate this number is very easy. Just divide the desired **Target Income** ($100,000) in annual terms by 0.04. The result is $2,500,000.

Assuming the savings will be invested in a 60/40 portfolio (60% stocks, 40% bonds), it will grow by 7.86% (the historical average*) annually, assuming this average rate will repeat year after year, for simulation purposes. Starting from $62,000, adding new savings of $4,970 per year (7% annual savings rate), and reinvesting all the earnings in the portfolio, how long would it take for this person to accumulate $2.5 million?

Answer: It would take **40 years** for this average person to accumulate $2.5 million under the Traditional 4% Rule.

* Historically, in the last 30 years, a 60/40 portfolio built with two Vanguard ETFs - VTI Vanguard Total Stock Market and BND Vanguard Totals Bond Market – where 60% was invested in VTI and 40% in BND, obtained an average annual return of 7.86%.

Note: Of course, no investment on the face of the Earth will earn a continuous, unchanged, and stable fixed return every year, let alone stocks and bonds. In some years, you will have much better returns, but in some other years, you will have worse returns, even negative ones. But for simulation purposes, we can assume it's fixed. But we must know the future cannot be predicted, so past returns do not guarantee future results. The same remarks will be applied to projections and simulations for any other type of investment throughout the book, including those used under the AFFF framework. For simplicity, I also assumed that annual savings of $4,970 are invested right in the middle of every year because the timing of deposits varies from person to person.

40 years is indeed a very long time. Most people won't even have the patience to wait that long, and the majority either don't believe in the plan or give up in the middle or before even trying. Now let's see how the AFFF would fare for the same person, under the same conditions and assumptions. To be fair, both methods will be compared under the exact same circumstances.

How would the same case fare under the AFFF framework?

As you know, the first principle of the AFFF calls for a multitude of assets and types of assets instead of a single type. The choice will depend on the context (economy and markets) and personal preferences. But for our demonstration purposes here, let's ignore the second principle of the AFFF for now, to keep it simple. Thus, I have selected a few asset choices for both stages. Let's test all of them under the AFFF framework against the Traditional 4% Rule, shall we?

Stage I – Capital Formation - Asset choices:

- 60/40 portfolio (historical average annual return: 7.86%)
- SPY/Cash - Outperform Level I* (historical average annual return: 11.80%)
- SSO/Cash - Outperform Level II* (historical average annual return: 30.10%)

Stage II – Income Production and Target Capital Lowering - Asset choices:

- A real estate portfolio (8% cap rate, leveraged at 80% LTV, 5%, 30-year).
- Autorun small businesses* (3x ODI multiple, leveraged at 50% LTV, 10%, 5-year).

* Outperform is a stock market investing method based on active daily risk management to protect against market crashes. The SPY and SSO are popular ETF's that track the S&P 500 and 2x S&P 500, respectively. I will describe Outperform and Autorun Small Businesses later in the book, more specifically in Chapter 5 and Chapter 9, respectively. ETF's ("Exchange-Traded Funds") are financial instruments conveniently designed by Wall Street similar to mutual funds with important differences: ETF's are typically cheaper than mutual funds, and they can be traded like a stock at any time. LTV of a loan is the percentage over the collateral's value the loan will cover.

Since we are simulating 3 types of assets in Stage I and 2 types of assets in Stage II, we will have 6 combinations of results, which I will show in a table format below.

THE ACCELERATED FINANCIAL FREEDOM FORMULA™
The Basic Framework – A Numerical Example

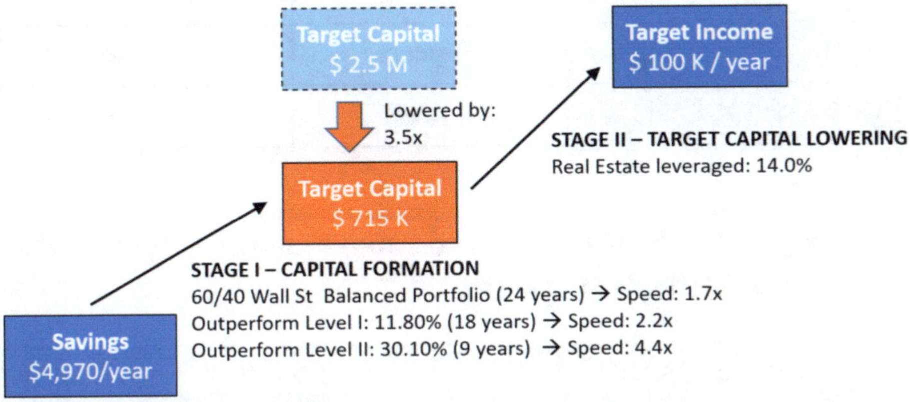

Note: Annual rates of return for Capital Formation (Stage I) used in this simulation are historical average annual returns for each of the instruments shown. Target Capital Lowering reduction rate is based on the use of real estate with cap rate 8%, loan rate 5%, 30Y, LTV 80%

Before I show you the results under the AFFF framework, let's just remember the time it would take to achieve financial freedom under the traditional method:

Traditional method (4% Rule): 60/40 Portfolio	40 years

See in the tables below the results of the simulation (projections) under the AFFF framework:

Number of years to achieve Financial Freedom:

Stage II asset➔ 🡻 Stage I assets	Real estate + leverage	Autorun Small Biz + leverage
60/40 Portfolio	24 years	12 years
Outperform Level I	18 years	10 years
Outperform Level II	9 years	5 years

AFFF Acceleration reached above normal speed from Traditional Methods (40 years):

Stage II assets ➔ 🡻 Stage I assets	Real estate + leverage	Autorun Small Biz + leverage
60/40 Portfolio	1.7x	3.3x
Outperform Level I	2.2x	4.0x
Outperform Level II	4.4x	8.0x

Let's look under the hood: how the AFFF works to achieve these results

➔ Let me illustrate the mechanism in slow motion so you can completely understand how it works. It's a **3-Step Sequence**:

STEP 1: Choose a value appreciation asset for Stage I and an income-producing asset for Stage II.

➔ Suppose you are this hypothetical average American and you chose Outperform Level I for Stage I and a real estate portfolio for Stage II.

For simulation purposes, we assume the Outperform Level I is growing at 11.8% annually and that the real estate portfolio pays an 8% cap rate, leveraged by an 80% LTV, 5%, 30-year loan from a bank.

STEP 2: Determine Target Capital given the asset chosen for Stage II and your desired Target Income.

➔ To calculate your new, reduced Target Capital, you will need to put the numbers in the generic real estate pro-forma (don't worry, you can download the Excel sheet from my author website for free. It's called the Flightplan.xlsx):

II. Real Estate Investing + OPM/E

Cap rate	8%
Loan rate	5%
Tenor (years)	30
LTV	80%
Leveraged Return	14.0%
Asset size	3,576,685
Target Capital	**715,337**
Req. money reduction	**57.2%**
Speed increase	**1.7x**
Monthly income	**8,333**
Annual income	**100,000**

Remember I discussed how to determine how much real estate property you must buy to deliver the income you want in Chapter 3: just divide your Target Income by the cash-on-cash return. Put the numbers in the Excel sheet and you will get cash-on-cash return (or Leverage Return) of 14% (see image). It's actually rounded up from 13.979%. Dividing $100,000 by this number, you get $715,337. This is your **Target Capital**.

You see, the bank is financing 80% of the real estate portfolio. The size of the portfolio would be $3.5 million, but you only need approximately $715,337 (budget for 10% more as safety margin) out of your own pocket. The bank would finance the rest ($2.8 million). That's the power of OPM/E in Stage II lowering the required Target Capital you would need from your own savings in Stage I (3rd principle of the AFFF).

I guess the question in your mind now is how do I buy a real estate investment property worth $3.5 million? Should I buy one property or multiple properties? This is a great question, but the answer is that it depends. If you can find one property and you qualify for the mortgage, great. If not, it can be 2, 3, or multiple smaller properties, instead; it doesn't matter. In practice, you will locate the best properties you can find (I teach people how to screen, find, analyze, verify (due diligence), negotiate, and buy properties in my Real Estate courses). Put in the cap rate (if multiple properties, aggregate them) and see how the numbers come out. You can invest in one or two multi-family buildings or even a portfolio of many single-family homes. If you choose the latter, there are portfolios for sale and portfolio loans available for investors, too. You may also combine physical real estate with paper real estate (deed of trust and mortgage notes – see Chapter 9). I teach how to invest in paper real estate in my online courses; if interested check out my author website).

And finally, make sure the last line shows the **Target Income** you are planning for. In this example, that is $100,000 net annual income flowing to you.

STEP 3: Estimate the number of years you will need in Stage I to reach the Target Capital

➔ Since OPM/E (your mortgage loan from the bank) reduced the Target Capital from $2.5 million to $715,337 for you, it made your trip to financial freedom shorter. You will only need your initial savings balance of $62,000 plus your annual savings of $4,970 per year to grow to $715,337.

If you chose Outperform Level I, which I will describe in more detail in a box in Chapter 5, as your asset for the job, you will be investing in the SPY ETF following Outperform's daily signals on when to invest and when to stay in cash. The Level

I averaged 11.8% annual return in the last 14 years. Assuming it will repeat every year (this is an assumption for planning purposes only because the reality will be different; it's normal for finance practitioners to assume the average return to repeat every year), you can see that it will take 18 years to reach Target Capital ($715,337). This is all calculated by the FlightPlan.xlsx spreadsheet you can download from my author website.

Once you reach Target Capital, you will transition from Stage I to Stage II. You will sell your SPY ETF holdings for cash. You are projected to have $749,221 in 18 years, give or take (again, this is just a plan, a simulation so you can visualize your possible future today). It will obviously depend on the market, which cannot be predicted. As soon as you have the Target Capital, or $749,221, you can start buying properties for the Stage II of your journey, which is to actually produce the income of $100,000 a year.

So, now you have it all calculated and demonstrated for you in 3 STEPS.

Interpretation of the results

Eighteen years to reach financial freedom for this **average** American may sound like too long for some or even too short for others. But compared to the traditional method based on the 4% Rule, which would require 40 years, under the same conditions and assumptions, the AFFF for this person would be twice as fast (estimated 2.2x faster).

Note that I'm not promising a specific speed, but by implementing the AFFF, you should be able to speed up your journey to financial freedom compared with traditional methods. Also note that for this simulation, I only used the 1st and 3rd principles of the AFFF, which is deploying two assets (one for each stage) and OPM. Furthermore, note that it's relative, not absolute, because it's going to be a different experience for everyone. I will show you a mathematical proof that the AFFF should be able to accelerate your journey to financial freedom by a factor of 2x to 10x, but individual results will vary greatly from person to person. But will I know how fast it will be for me, you may be asking. The exact length of time to achieve your financial freedom will vary from person to person and will depend on a few factors. The most obvious and important ones are:

- **Your departure**: your starting point and personal circumstances, such as income, savings rate, wealth, etc. are very important. People with higher income, savings, savings rate, and wealth will invariably have an advantage, like an early lead in the journey.
- **Your destination**: the amount of Target Income you want to achieve also matters. The higher the Target Income, naturally, the longer your journey.
- **Your execution**: your commitment and determination to change your life and implement the steps in your personal AFFF journey. Quality of execution is a key determinant of results in any undertaking in life, isn't it?
- **External factors**: you don't control them, but they can affect your speed. For example, economic conditions at the start and throughout the journey will help or hinder your journey. Just like in a rocket launch, where winds, temperature, and other climatic conditions may help or hinder the rocket from moving faster, the same applies here. It's inevitable, but the AFFF will guide you through to make the best of your journey even if you encounter headwinds.

If you had chosen different assets, the results would have been very different, too, of course. As you can see, this is the power of choice. Those who have choices have power.

We will detail each of these factors further in the book. But even 2x the speed is still a fantastic deal, let alone even faster speeds. I dare say that virtually anyone who is committed to following the AFFF and executing the method with determination will experience some degree of acceleration from 2x and up. That's how confident I am in the method.

A great analogy would be a rocket launch for a journey to the Moon. The travel time will depend on the distance between the Earth and the Moon (you want to launch when the Earth and the Moon are at the closest distance from each other), the thrust your rocket engine produces, whether you have boosters, what kind of fuel, and of course, how much money is available, because all of this will depend on the budget NASA has allocated for the project. It will also depend on external factors (what I call "context"), such as atmospheric conditions (temperature, winds, etc.) and luck. These external factors, you can't control. Often external factors can seriously delay and even cancel a launch. Therefore, just like space travel where every NASA launch is not exactly the same, a journey to financial freedom will vary from person to person, and everyone's speed may be very different. But still, what the AFFF can do for you is to accelerate the speed you would have reached with traditional methods without the AFFF.

Wrap up your understanding of the AFFF in comparison with Traditional Methods

In conclusion, let's just quickly wrap up the presentation of the AFFF with a visual contrasting the difference between the methods, so it becomes very clear to you.

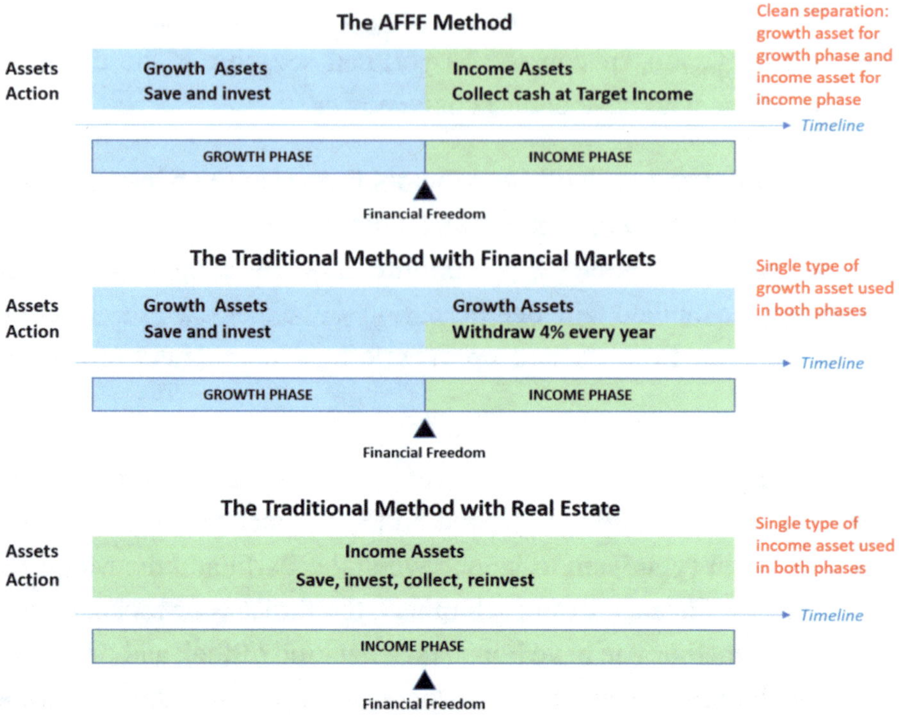

Notice that, unlike the 4% Rule method used by financial markets practitioners, the AFFF is made up of two stages – Stages I and II. The 4% Rule uses stocks and bonds to grow savings and then withdraws 4% annually from it as income. I think this is very problematic and inefficient (remember the "Cow and Milk" Analogy I made in Chapter 2). Stocks and bonds are good assets for value appreciation (growth), not income. Only income can effectively offset a person's daily living expenses and lifestyle.

Real estate is much better for income generation. So is a small business. As I said earlier, you can achieve financial freedom with income-generation assets alone. But this works best for those who have already saved enough money earlier and can afford to buy properties or small businesses outright. These folks may even skip the growth phase. But for a comprehensive framework that works for everyone, the AFFF optimized the process separating the journey into two stages:

- Stage I's goal is to grow your savings – choose the best value appreciation type of assets.
- Stage II's goal is generate income for you – choose the best income-producing assets.

This separation into two individual stages is one of the keys to give the AFFF an edge because it allowed us to maximize the effect of each type of asset. Let each asset do what it does best! This is a direct consequence of being a multi-asset method instead of a single asset method like the other two. In fact, the AFFF combines the best of the other two and leaves out the worse of them. To understand why, how about another analogy? Imagine two teams competing in a triathlon. Team A has only one triathlon athlete. That individual is very good at swimming, good at running, and okay at cycling. Team B has 3 specialists, each with their own field of specialization (swimming, running, and cycling). Which team do you think will have the best chance at winning the race?

Remember: if you want to accelerate your way to financial freedom, efficiency is really a big deal! You can't afford inefficient methods. Every bit of efficiency you can optimize in your process will make a massive difference over time.

Author's Side Note: This book is structured to provide readers a gradual progress from the basic idea of the novel method to finance concepts and a deeper dive into actual implementation. I will hold **online workshops** to help not only with conveying important concepts, but especially with the practical aspects of the AFFF method's implementation. Sign up for my free newsletter on my author website and you will be notified when these educational events will occur.

CHAPTER 5

5. How you can apply each of the four AFFF principles

Principle #1- Multi-Asset Type Approach: The power of deploying multiple asset classes

Traditional methods are mostly unidimensional, I mean, focused on one single asset type. Most financial freedom proponents are either on the financial markets camp (using traditional financial products, techniques, and methods) or on the real estate camp (real estate investors usually abhor the stock market). As I said earlier, I see 3 major groups out there:

The Real Estate Camp: This crowd lives and breathes real estate all day long. These folks are typically allergic to the stock market for its 'resemblance to nothing more than a giant cassino.' Real estate is indeed a very powerful asset class for both income production and wealth buildup. It is also loaded with incredible tax breaks and allows for easy leveraging. Plus, most success stories do happen here with people from all walks of life achieving financial freedom. But there are problems with investing only in real estate:

- Real estate requires higher entry tickets (minimum investment amounts).
- For most people, it will take a long time to save enough money to get started.

- Real estate appreciation is generally slow compared to financial assets.
- It involves over-concentration of risk in a single type of asset and its market cycles.

The Financial Markets Camp: Generally, this crowd is as diverse as the real estate camp. One important subgroup tends to be more sophisticated, skilled, and less risk-averse than the rest. Their preferred investments are stocks, bonds, options, and even annuities. Another large subgroup comprises those who, for lack of time or skills (or both), decided to simply outsource the management of their finances to a third party (e.g. bankers, money managers, and financial advisors). Financial instruments are much more convenient to invest in than real estate. You can trade stocks, ETF's, options, etc., with just a click of a mouse from the comfort of your home. For those who outsource their investment decisions, it's on autopilot or just a phone call away. For these folks, it may be easy, hands off (almost 100% passive), but what about the results? Investing in financial markets alone for financial freedom has problems too:

- Stocks are best for growth, not income (dividend rates are too small).
- Selling stocks and bonds for income is a bad idea (remember the "Cow & Milk" Analogy discussed in Chapter 2). Also, what if the timing is bad to sell? Expenses work like clockwork; markets don't.
- Financial assets require very large amounts because the volatility causes uncertainty and makes them harder to use as collateral for OPM leverage.
- What about retirement security? The longevity risk problem (outliving your money) is not solved.

The 'Others' Camp: This is the smallest group with a very diverse group of individuals, who don't principally belong to any of the other camps. In the 'Others' camp, an important subgroup is composed of entrepreneurs focused on their own businesses. They prefer to reinvest the bulk of their earnings back into their ventures rather than investing in something else, except for diversification purposes. Also included in this broad group called "the others" are folks who invest in non-cashflow producing assets like land, precious metals (gold, silver, etc.), fine arts, collectibles, commodity contracts, etc., and even cryptocurrencies. Except for business entrepreneurship (starting or acquiring one), which can be used for financial freedom, the other types of assets won't be very useful for purposes of financial freedom (they don't generate income or cashflow; they're purely speculative for growth). In theory, they could be used in Stage I - Capital Formation for acceleration purposes, but they are very risky instruments and require highly specific knowledge.

The problem with belonging to a specific camp is that if the stock market or the real estate market is in trouble, you will have no viable alternative options. Markets operate in cycles, and getting the timing right is absolutely crucial. What if the market you invest in is overvalued and about to decline? Being unidimensional with a single asset type, you will have no other choices if the market moment happens to be wrong. As a result, you become too dependent on the market. Entering or exiting the market at the wrong times will slow down your journey to financial freedom. Those who were fortunate enough to ride a bull market will achieve financial freedom faster than those who start during a bear market. It should not be like that, in my opinion.

So, what's the best asset class to accelerate your journey to financial freedom? You may have guessed by now. It's **ALL of the above!** The AFFF is a multi-asset class approach. If you're serious about accelerating your financial freedom 2x-10x faster, you will need to have the entire spectrum of investment instruments available to you.

Below is an overview of how systems are connected for your journey to financial freedom under the AFFF framework, using an analogy of a space mission rocket launch:

- **The Growth Engine**: delivers capital appreciation to grow your capital to reach Target Capital faster (Stage I – Capital Formation).
- **The Income Engine**: produces income, your Target Income, to sustain your financial freedom with the extra push provided by the boosters (Stage II – Income Production and Target Capital Lowering).
- **Booster 1**: accelerates your journey with OPM/E (E stands for external sources).
- **Booster 2**: accelerates your journey with OPM/I (I stands for internal sources).

In the spaceship analogy, the engines will be powered by a variety of different fuels (assets), which can be chosen from the menu of assets below.

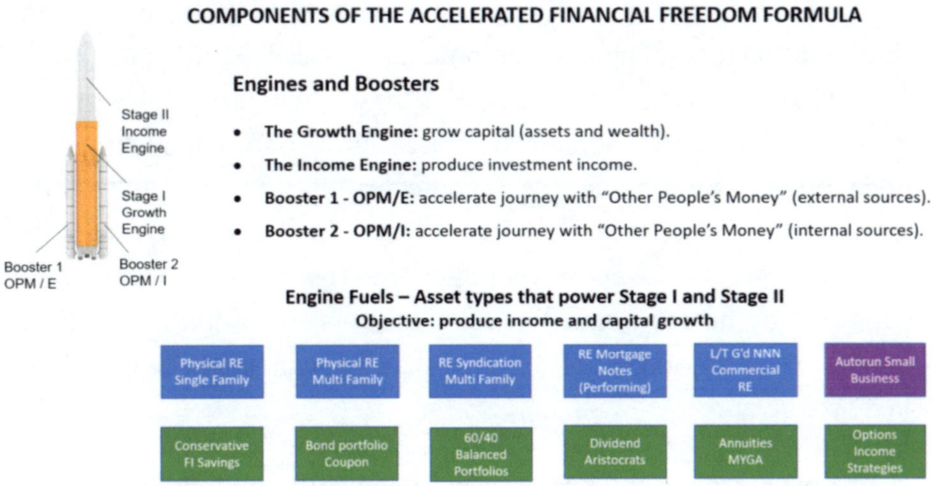

How do you choose assets? Each type of asset will have its unique characteristics, risk-return profile, and pros and cons, among other important features. The choice of asset will depend on the context at the moment of your decision (by context, I mean the economy and markets), and of course, your personal preferences, needs and goals. Other important considerations for making choices are the degree of passiveness (how much work and time it demands from you), how easy and familiar to you, etc. We will help you make your own choices later when you prepare your own AFFF Flightplan in Chapter 8.

Stage I assets (best for value appreciation) are indicated in green boxes. Stage II assets (best for income generation) are indicated in blue and purple boxes. Check the diagrams below for details.

How to choose assets: you will have to balance which features are most important for you. Look at each one of them: money required, yield, passiveness, easiness, income stability, and appreciation potential. For example, if you are a very busy professional and don't have much time to learn or manage investments, you may want to look for assets that are more passive and easier for starters. But if you wish to learn and really optimize your results, seriously speeding up your financial freedom, you may want to ignore these two features and focus on yield and appreciation potential instead. Yield is the rate of return of the cashflow for income purposes. Another very important consideration is risk. Some people are more comfortable taking risks than others, so look at the income stability feature. Give more preference to assets that are safer if you are a very conservative investor. Riskier assets have higher returns. The money required feature may be important for new investors, who don't have much money to get started. If this is you, you may want to check the money required feature.

To help you select the best assets for you, first review the menu of commonly used assets below. To make a decision, you will need to think about each of these aspects and how they fit your needs and circumstances:

- **Amount of money required**: some assets require larger amounts than others. Often the price tag of an asset may become a barrier to entry in that market. Depending on the amount of savings you have available to make investments, this can be an important consideration for you. However, don't be discouraged if you can't afford to buy the asset now. As you work through Stage I of the AFFF, you will eventually be able to afford it. If this is your case, you just need to change the order of asset acquisitions in your plan.
- **Yield**: this is more important for Stage II, as the rate of return for the income the asset produces on average helps you have an idea about the asset's cash generation power. Just remember that the higher the yield, the faster you would accumulate earnings, but higher yields come with higher risks as well. So, you will need to find the best balance between return and risk for you. Yield is a more useful measure for Stage II assets

because they are chosen for their ability to produce income or cash flow to you.

- **Passiveness**: most of you are not professional investors and many of you don't even have much time to dedicate to your investments. If this is your case, you should look for assets that are more passive in nature, not requiring too much of your time. But for those who do have time to dedicate to their investments, this is not a big issue. A more active type of investment requiring more of your time will likely give you better results than more passive ones.
- **Easiness**: people have different levels of knowledge and experience with different types of assets. But some assets are easier to understand and to learn the basics than others. It's always imperative that you only invest in things you can understand. If you want to invest in anything you don't know very well, you must acquire proper education first.
- **Stability of the income**: this is more relevant for Stage II. Some people can deal better with fluctuations in the income streams than others. For those who can't, the stability of the income streams may be an important consideration. To mitigate disruptions caused by income fluctuations, which do happen, consider a little higher Target Income in your projections (e.g., 10% or 15% higher) as a margin against potential fluctuations, or choose more stable assets.
- **Appreciation potential**: this is more important for Stage I as you are quickly building up assets to reach your Target Capital. The higher the appreciation potential, the faster you will arrive at your Target Capital. However, bear in mind that higher returns always come with higher risks and volatility. You will need to strike a good balance between high return and a level

of risk that is tolerable for you. This is absolutely important as you embark on this journey.

To make the right choices will always involve making tradeoffs across the above attributes. I show you why. Imagine an "ideal" asset. How should it rank across the five attributes?

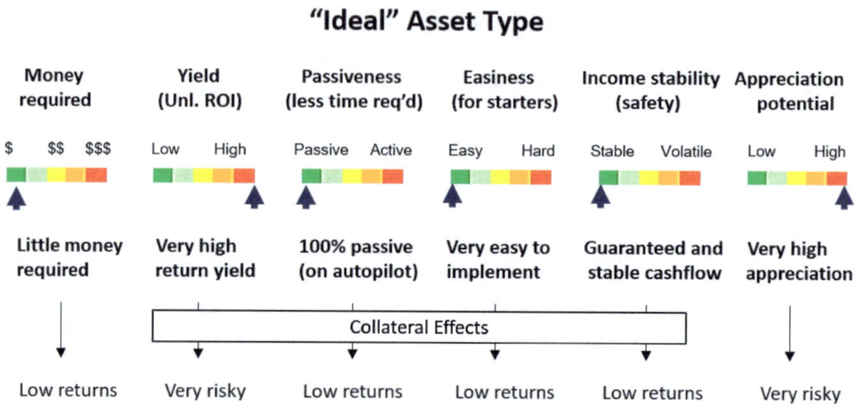

If it existed, the "ideal" asset should require the least possible amount of money to invest, produce the highest income possible (highest ROI), be 100% passive (require zero work), be super-easy to understand and to implement, be 100% safe, stable, and guaranteed, and finally have a very high appreciation potential. Such an asset, if it existed in the real world, would be really ideal. Unfortunately, it doesn't exist. Generally, investments requiring small amounts to invest, investments that are close to 100% passive, investments that are easy to implement, and investments that are the safest and most stable have one common undesirable collateral effect: they have low returns. On the other hand, investments that have the highest returns (yield and/or appreciation potential) also have their common undesirable collateral effect: they are very risky. That is why this "ideal" asset does not exist. But that is fine; we don't need the perfect asset to be successful. We only need to select the assets that are the best fit for each one of us according to our most important attributes.

In summary, choice of assets is very personal. How many should you choose? At this point, I would start by ranking them in order of preference. The final choice will depend on the 2nd principle of the AFFF, which is the analysis of the context (state of the economy and markets). You will want to time the asset choice correctly with the market for maximum chance of success.

Stage I Asset Choices
(Value appreciation assets for growth)

Stage II Asset Choices
(Income-generation assets)

This list of asset types is not exhaustive. There are more out there. I only listed the most commonly known and used. Note also that yield and appreciation numbers are subject to **change at any time** and do constantly evolve. By the time you read this book, numbers will have changed from the time I wrote them. All numbers in an economy are constantly changing. Use them as a reference in relative terms, to compare one asset with another.

Just bear in mind is that Stage I requires assets that favor growth (value appreciation or capital gains), and Stage II requires assets that favor income (cashflow) and are leverageable with OPM. The reason is that during Stage I, you want to accumulate the most capital the fastest way possible. In Stage II, you want your assets producing income for you. With that distinction in mind, I offer some suggestions for assets to be used in Stage I and Stage II. Again, this list is not exhaustive; it's given so you understand the logic. The green boxes are financial assets, the blue boxes are real estate assets, and the purple boxes are businesses.

Connecting Stage I and Stage II Assets

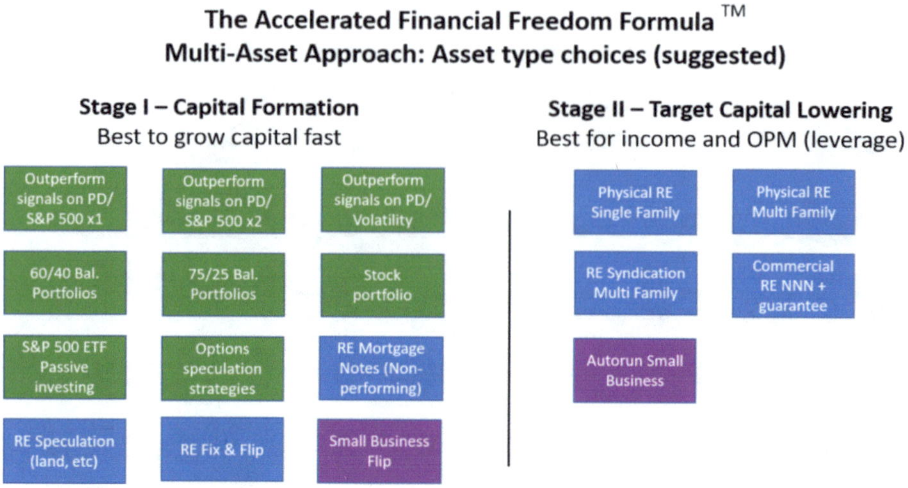

Asset choices for Conservative Investors

Some people are naturally very conservative investors. They cannot tolerate risks very well. If that is their comfort zone, it is perfectly normal. Everyone has a different personality that must be respected. They should understand that lower risks generally mean lower returns, which, in turn, mean slower growth and a longer time to reach financial freedom. Again, this is perfectly fine. Often, it's the conservative investors who arrive at their intended destination and sometimes before the more aggressive investors. This may happen because higher risks may cause unexpected setbacks, which can delay their journey. (Just a side note: the Outperform project, explained below, was developed exactly to prevent these unexpected setbacks as much as possible). Everyone must find their point of equilibrium to balance desired return (and speed) with risks. For conservative investors, I offer some asset suggestions below:

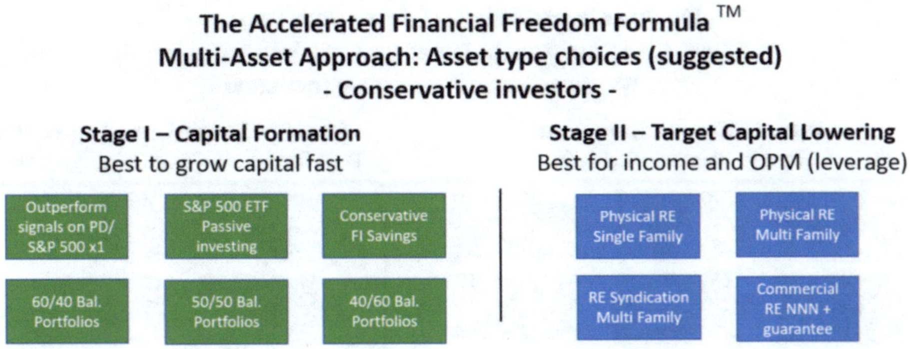

Asset Choices for Moderate and Aggressive Investors

On the other hand, moderate and aggressive investors can tolerate running higher risks for a higher return. They understand that risk and return are both two sides of the same coin; risk and return are bound together tightly. These investors feel confident enough to let go of some safety in exchange for a higher return. They won't feel too anxious every time their stocks face headwinds and lose value. If you have this investor profile, either moderate or aggressive, you may choose assets that have a higher risk-return profile. A higher return may potentially make your journey much faster. But as I commented earlier, you may also encounter headwinds delaying your trip. Let me also offer some suggested assets for the moderate and aggressive investors:

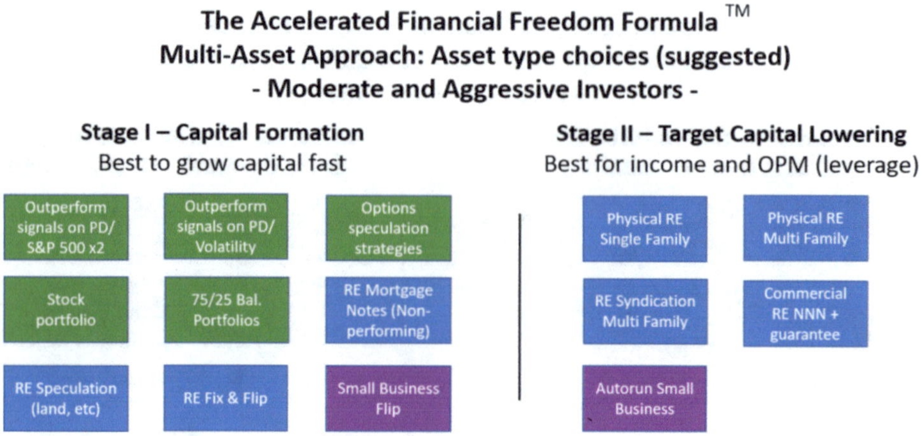

To conclude this topic, imagine you're launching a mission to Mars, and you know that *failure is not an option* (famously said by Gene Kranz, NASA's legendary flight director for Apollo missions). Would you build only one rocket, use only one type of fuel, train only one single crew of astronauts, and launch on a single pre-scheduled day? Of course, you wouldn't. You want to be flexible, preparing for all situations you can anticipate (and for situations you can't anticipate too!), and maximize all tools and technology at your disposal, would you not? Rockets and modern airplanes are designed with many backup systems built in to make sure you arrive safe and sound at your destination.

If that's so, why don't people use a multi-asset approach in their journey to financial freedom? Here is why. Over-specialization for some. Lack of proper financial education for others. In your journey to financial freedom, you will certainly face headwinds and roadblocks, so you need to be flexible and have options, just like a team sports coach will have players on the bench ready for action at any time depending on what's going on in the field.

What is Outperform?

The Outperform (renamed RISP 500™ Project) - You may be wondering about the Outperform Signals I suggested as alternative assets for Stage I. The Outperform Signals is a project I started with a few partners, who were distinguished, highly technical traders and quantitative analysts ("quants") I had the pleasure of working with in my professional life in trading floors. After the 2008 Subprime Housing and Financial Crisis market crash, when people from all walks of life lost a lot of money in their 401k accounts and stock portfolios, the seeds of the Outperform project were born. The idea was to avoid another 2008 by developing an algorithm to crunch real-time data on markets to measure risks. The stock market is not isolated but intimately inter-connected with the rest of the ecosystem: bond markets, currency markets, capital flows, economic variables, and the derivatives markets. The relationships between these markets and variables, including the VIX* and VIX futures, can be measured and combined to produce a consolidated measure of risks – the RISP 500™ – that may give us advanced warning the stock market may be about to turn seriously by signaling elevation of risks in the markets.

** The VIX, aka. "the fear index," is a measure of future expected volatility in the stock market. The VIX alone is not very useful to provide warning signs or to be used as a timing tool; however, it's an important piece of the puzzle when analyzed together with other indicators.*

Outperform (the name of the algorithm) works like checking the weather every morning before going out. If the RISP 500™ indicates low or normal risks in the markets, I can confidently be holding risky assets (stocks, SPY, SSO, etc.) because the odds of losing are relatively small. But if it indicates elevated risks, the odds of winning vs. losing becomes unfavorable to me, so I should sell them and hold cash or a bond ETF (e.g., the IEF) and wait for a better moment to return to the market. Of course, the market fluctuates, and small losses are normally acceptable. The goal is to avoid big losses, like serious corrections and crashes that can wipe out accounts or which may take a long time for recovery. For example, the 2000 internet bubble burst market crash took 7 years to recover (i.e., just to break even!), and the 2008 Crisis market crash took 6 years just to return to where it was before the crash. These signals are produced once a day around 12 pm ET and distributed by email to subscribers (there is a small subscription fee for live signals). For the user, it takes less than 2 minutes a day to check the signal just like checking the weather. Only on days when the market is volatile will the user make a trade; most of the time, the user does nothing, so it's very easy, passive, and convenient for everyone. Outperform issues 3 levels of signals on a daily basis:

Level I (renamed Strategy 1): signals when to invest in the SPY ETF (S&P 500 x1) or to stay in Cash.

Level II (renamed Strategy 3): signals when to invest in the SSO ETF (S&P 500 x2) or stay in Cash or IEF (bond ETF).

The PD/M2x strategy: PD stands for "Protect Downside." The downside protection is provided by the daily signals. If the market turns dangerous, users will be notified by the RISP 500™. M2x means market return doubled (S&P 500 return x2). PD/M2x capitalizes on that protection to be bolder at investing. Think about this: if you are confident the market is bullish (risks are low or normal) in a day (as measured by the RISP 500™), you can be bolder to bet in a riskier asset – the SSO, which returns twice the S&P 500 for the day. It's just like a sports team that has a solid defense: its offensive players are freed to play bolder strategies because if attacked, they have confidence in their defense.

More information on Outperform (renamed RISP 500™) can be found on this website: https://www.Engineering-Finance.com. Obviously, this is not a crystal ball and markets are unpredictable. But it is a system that has a solid technical background and has been tested for over a decade. There is a small fee for subscribing to the live signals issued once a day around lunch time in New York.

Principle #2 – Timing investments to the context (economy & market cycles)

The power of timing investments right to the pace of the economy & market cycles

Borrowing the previous sports analogy sounds like a good idea because a coach will choose the right players from the bench for the game according to what the team encounters in the field. Or the war analogy also works. In war, as a commander, you must deploy the right weapons according to what you see happening in the battlefield and your strategy to win. It's the exact same idea Principle #2 of the AFFF is proposing to you.

The economic context, or investment environment (level of inflation, interest rates, etc.) is not under our control. It is an external factor. What works well in certain conditions often doesn't work well in other conditions. For example, in high inflation scenarios, real estate and stocks work better than fixed income investments. In a fast-growing economy, stocks tend to jump ahead of real estate and fixed income. But in a recession, multifamily real estate tends to work better than commercial real estate and single-family home investments. You get the idea! As the saying goes, *you can't control the wind, but you can adjust the sails* for maximum performance and results. The 2nd principle of the AFFF is all about adjusting sails in response to winds for maximum performance and results.

I will present a series of charts showing the past history and cycles of boom and bust on a long-term perspective. Everything seems to move in cycles. Imagine a pendulum swinging from side to side. You can think of economic cycles as a giant pendulum swinging from growth to recession and back to growth in a never-ending motion over the course of decades. Asset prices certainly move in cycles too. The pendulum of market cycles exhibits similar behavior. That is why it is so important to recognize in which stage of the cycle an asset rests before considering buying or selling it. The best moment to buy an asset is generally when the pendulum of the market cycle for the asset is moving or transitioning from market pessimism (or what we call "bear" market) to market optimism (or what we call "bull" market). The worst moment to buy an asset is when the pendulum is swinging in the opposite direction. The best and worst times to sell assets are the exact opposite from the best and worst times to buy such assets. Don't confuse market fluctuations with cycles. For price changes to define cycles, the trend must change in a significant way. I will give you an example with the stock market.

The Stock Market - The U.S. stock market had a long series of positive return years since the bottom of the 2008 Subprime Crisis market crash until 2021, making it a 13-year long bull market. See table below. During this long streak of up years, there were two events that brought the market severely down: the first occurred in 2018, when the Fed raised rates at the same time of the U.S.-China trade war, causing a market meltdown. The second was the Coronavirus crash in 2020. But these events were short-lived and hadn't really altered the bullish trend until 2022. The Coronavirus crash lasted just a few months. In 2022, it became clear the bull market was finally over, not just because of stock price declines but because the economy was facing significant headwinds, with the Federal Reserve aggressively hiking the country's interest rates. So, there you had a cycle. Cycles usually last years, decades, but can be shorter or longer depending on the entire context.

Check out the U.S. stock market up and down years since 1928 in the table below.

U.S. Stock Market - S&P 500 Index Total Returns (1928 - 2022)									
Year	Return	Year	Return	Year	Return	Year	Return	Year	Return
1928	43.8%	1947	5.2%	1966	-10.0%	1985	31.2%	2004	10.9%
1929	-8.3%	1948	5.7%	1967	23.8%	1986	18.5%	2005	4.9%
1930	-25.1%	1949	18.3%	1968	10.8%	1987	5.8%	2006	15.8%
1931	-43.8%	1950	30.8%	1969	-8.2%	1988	16.6%	2007	5.5%
1932	-8.6%	1951	23.7%	1970	3.6%	1989	31.7%	2008	-37.0%
1933	50.0%	1952	18.2%	1971	14.2%	1990	-3.1%	2009	26.5%
1934	-1.2%	1953	-1.2%	1972	18.8%	1991	30.5%	2010	15.1%
1935	46.7%	1954	52.6%	1973	-14.3%	1992	7.6%	2011	2.1%
1936	31.9%	1955	32.6%	1974	-25.9%	1993	10.1%	2012	16.0%
1937	-35.3%	1956	7.4%	1975	37.0%	1994	1.3%	2013	32.4%
1938	29.3%	1957	-10.5%	1976	23.8%	1995	37.6%	2014	13.7%
1939	-1.1%	1958	43.7%	1977	-7.0%	1996	23.0%	2015	1.4%
1940	-10.7%	1959	12.1%	1978	6.5%	1997	33.4%	2016	12.0%
1941	-12.8%	1960	0.3%	1979	18.5%	1998	28.6%	2017	21.8%
1942	19.2%	1961	26.6%	1980	31.7%	1999	21.0%	2018	-4.4%
1943	25.1%	1962	-8.8%	1981	-4.7%	2000	-9.1%	2019	31.5%
1944	19.0%	1963	22.6%	1982	20.4%	2001	-11.9%	2020	18.4%
1945	35.8%	1964	16.4%	1983	22.3%	2002	-22.1%	2021	28.7%
1946	-8.4%	1965	12.4%	1984	6.1%	2003	28.7%	2022	-18.1%

The chart below makes this point clearer. You can spot the cycles visually. They will repeat. As an investor in the stock market, you need to pay attention to what is currently going on and know what the current trend is. Of course, there will be lots of opinions out there, often contradicting one another. When in doubt about what to believe, choose the most conservative approach.

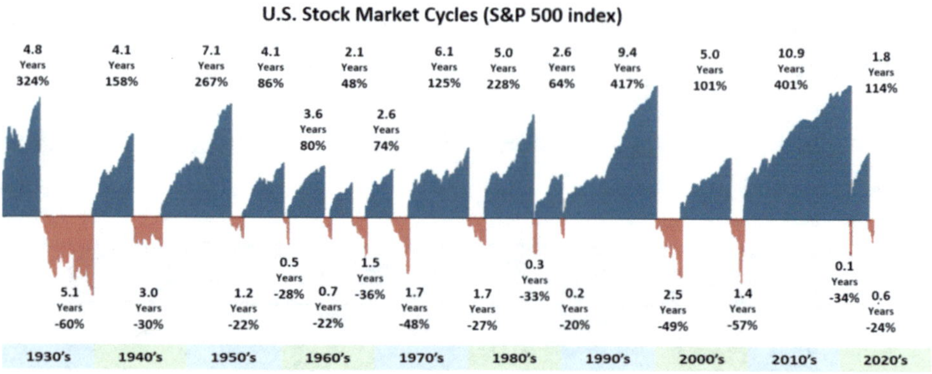

When you look at the evolution of the stock market prices in a price chart, especially under a very long-term perspective, you often can't see cycles clearly. See chart below of the S&P 500 since the 1880's.

This chart helps to put in perspective the spectacular growth of the U.S. stock market since World War II. One thing to be careful of is whether this extraordinary force will continue into the future and at what kind of strength. Here are a few things to think about. After World War II, the U.S. became the economic engine and the superpower of the world. The U.S. dollar became the hegemonic currency in the world, giving the country an unparalleled world economic power. All countries needed to buy the U.S. dollar for trade payments and reserves. This in turn projected American companies to dominate the entire world. As a result, the American stock market responded in kind. But how about the future? Will the U.S. hegemony continue, or will there be challenges? Since the last decade, we witnessed the rise of China, India, and other emerging economies. The G-7 countries, which includes the United States, no longer represent more than half of the world economy as they once did. It declined to 30%. That is why the G-20 was introduced. The G-20 accounts for 80% of the world's GDP now. Do the math, the remaining 14 G-20 emerging economies (non-G-7) are now making 50% of the world's economy. This trend is projected to continue. The 2018 trade war with China and attempts to decouple the two largest economies of the world, de-globalization, and disruption of global supply chains are probably ending the long period of low inflation and interest rates near zero in the U.S., so the emerging new world of the 21st century may look different from what we have become accustomed to in the last 70 years. Higher inflation and increased competition with other global emerging players may or may not sustain the stock market the same way it did in the past. This could be a fundamental tectonic shift that won't play out overnight, but over the course of years and decades. Therefore, investors must exercise caution and invest wisely. Risk management is absolutely paramount. The Outperform project was born exactly for this purpose. I will teach techniques in my online courses, and people may also subscribe to Outperform daily signals to help protect their investments from serious headwinds and crashes.

The Real Estate Market – Cycles in real estate may be slower but they do matter just the same. If you hear real estate pundits preaching that every day is a good day to buy real estate, it is not true. Real estate prices don't move every minute like stock prices, but they do move, and yes, they can and do go down at times. Real estate prices move slowly, and as a result, real estate cycles may be very long, spanning from years to decades. Residential real estate prices depend on a number of factors, such as demographics, population moves/migration, local economy, pace of construction, land availability, political factors, and mortgage rates, among many others. See a historical price index chart tracked by Case-Shiller's methodology by S&P Global below:

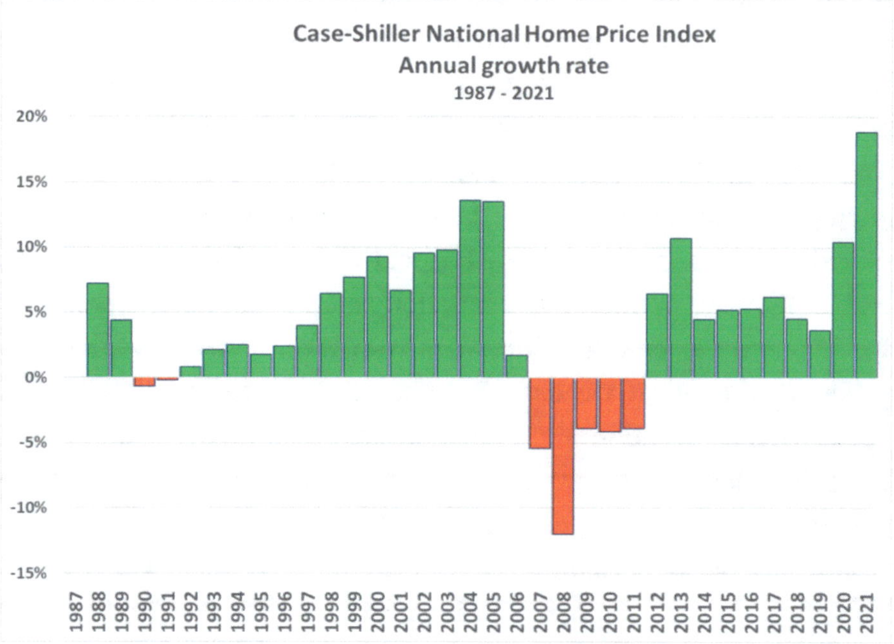

You can find more housing price charts at the S&P Case Shiller Composite Housing Index website. They have a national index and also a 10-city index and a 20-city index.

As you can see, home prices at the national level have experienced long periods of growth. They've been broken by the 2008 Subprime Housing and Financial Crisis, and more recently in 2022, after an explosive growth since the 2020 pandemic. The first bubble (burst in 2008) was fueled by an uncontrolled speculation and credit expansion. The second bubble (burst in 2022) was fueled by an expansion of money in circulation promoted by the Federal Reserve's zero interest rate policy and excessive money printing. Much of this excess money found its way to the housing market, the stock market, the bond market, cryptocurrencies, etc., inflating bubbles everywhere. Some call it "Bubble Everything." The housing market is going through a correction in 2022, not a crash.

But it doesn't mean you should stay away from real estate because, as you know, there is not one single national market for real estate like stocks, but many sub-markets across the country. By nature, real estate is a very fragmented market. Every location has its own price dynamics and cycles. Every state and municipality may be at different points in the cycle at any given moment. While some places may be experiencing expansion, other places may already be in decline. The granularity of this market fragmentation often surprises me. In New York City, for example, even a block or a specific building may have a unique pricing dynamic different from the rest of the city. Real estate is really a very local business. See the chart below. It shows where each metropolitan area across the country was siting along the cycle curve in 2014. It gives you a visual example like a "snapshot" of the real estate market at that moment evidencing what I meant by different locations being at different points in the cycle at any given moment. This granularity actually creates opportunities for us, investors.

Example of a market snapshot:

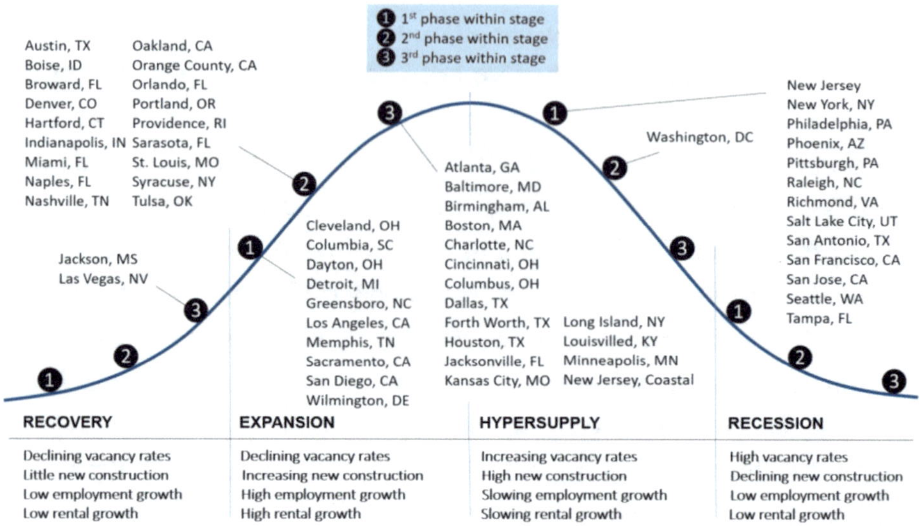

Example of a market snapshot taken in 2014. Information source: Integra Realty Resources, Inc.

In the chart, you can see the cycle subdivided in 4 stages: recovery, expansion, hyper-supply, and recession. You also see a bunch of cities at each of these stages simultaneously, although many of them tend to follow the national trend. This is because macroeconomic factors such as interest rates, inflation, and GDP growth affect us all, regardless of location.

So, here I would like to share my opinion about a very common belief, actually a "word of wisdom" that is very disseminated out there. You must have certainly heard this already many times. It goes like this: "*You should only invest near where you live.*" Many people believe in that advice. My personal opinion is that it only works for someone who wants to be a weekend landlord renting a few units and personally managing them. As an investor, I don't want to be restricted to where I live. What if where I live is a great place to live but a terrible place to invest? What if it's at an unfavorable point in the cycle right now? What should I do? Sit down quietly and wait? That is my reason for rejecting that advice.

To invest from afar does present a set of challenges. You must set up a system to do your pre-acquisition due diligence and select a reliable local professional property manager. I have a checklist to screen property managers through an interview with them face to face in their office. You also want to see their work in action. This is an important step that cannot be overlooked because the quality of their work will directly reflect on your ROI. I always try to find at least 2 or 3 good property managers and sign with the best one, so in case it doesn't work out with my top choice, I have already interviewed a back-up and won't need to travel to the far location again. I will provide my own checklists to my students in my online courses and mentorship program.

How long is each cycle in real estate? Historically, it ranges from 8 to 15 years. Each stage lasts on average 3 to 5 years. But, of course, it is not the same everywhere in the country. On the East Coast and West Coast of the continental United States, where most of the population and economic activity are concentrated, cycles are shorter than in the less populated interior of the country. People live where the jobs are. This has profound implications on the real estate market. Because of the difference in cycle lengths, you will have locations across the country spread out in all stages of the cycle at any given time.

Another great feature of real estate investing is that even if the current point in the cycle is not favorable for a "buy low, sell high" strategy, there are other appropriate strategies you can use. For example, take a look at the chart below. In each of the 4 stages in the cycle, you can see 4 different strategies you can employ at each stage. The most profitable of all, with the power to make millionaires, is buying at the beginning of the recovery stage, when prices are still low, and sell at the peak of the market at the end of the next stage. Who said timing doesn't matter?

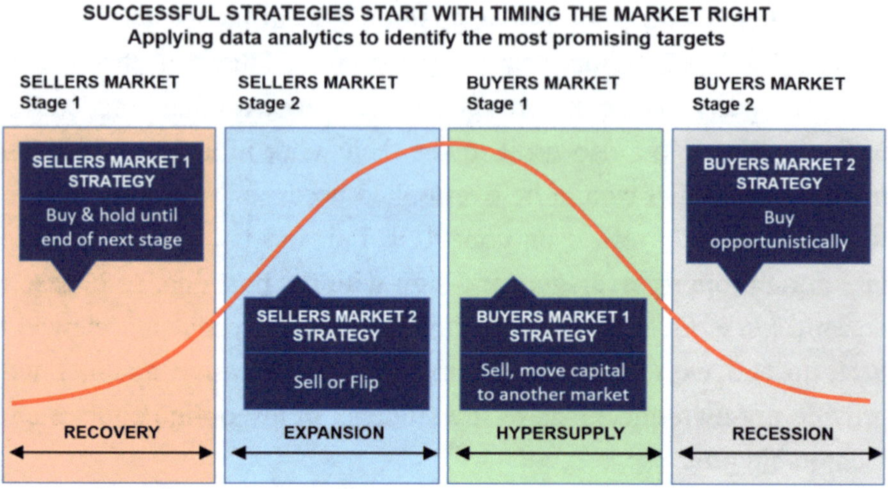

Credits: AnalyticRealty.com

The Bond Market and Interest Rates – Bonds are a complex topic to be reasonably covered in this book. Bonds are also not the preferred asset to speed up your financial freedom unless you are very conservative. In addition, bonds may be quite risky. Bonds are often used in combination with stocks to reduce a little bit of the risk of the combined portfolio. Some people believe bonds hedge stocks. This is not true. Sometimes they may move in opposite directions creating the feeling that they are inversely correlated to each other, hedging each other, but this is not always the case. In 2022, for example, they moved in the same direction: down. The result is that balanced portfolios of stocks and bonds suffered, no matter if your composition was 60/40 or 40/60. But bonds do soften the risks of a portfolio of only stocks. Here I will focus more on interest rates that affect everything in the economy. But I will talk about a few basic things related to bonds.

The first thing to know is that most bonds are fixed rate bonds. It's best for debt issuers because it's less risky for them. For fixed rate bonds, the price of the bond moves in the opposite direction from the economy's interest rates. The reason is simple. A bond is just a stream of future payments. If interest rates in the economy go up and the bond pays a fixed rate, the bond would become unattractive for potential buyers in the bond market. As a result, the price of fixed rate bonds will have to fall to adjust. The reverse is true when interest rates go up. That is why fixed rate bond prices always move in the opposite direction of interest rates.

Depending on the bond issuer, it may be classified as a treasury bond (if the issuer is the U.S. federal government), a municipal bond (states and municipalities), or a corporate bond (companies). The treasury bond market is huge, and it's considered the safest because the federal government has the power to "print" U.S. dollars to pay for its debt obligations, and the U.S. dollar is the world reserve currency. Also called "treasuries," maturities can span from just a few days to 30 years. The shortest maturity treasuries are called bills. The intermediate maturities from 2 years to 10 years are called notes. Longer maturities above 10 years and up to 30 years are called bonds.

The 10-year treasury note yield (or rate) is an interest rate commonly used as a benchmark. For example, mortgage rates are based on it. See chart below. Notice that since the 1980's, the yield has consistently dropped. It has actually been a 40-year bull market for bonds. Remember that in the bond world, interest rates and prices move in oppose directions. But in 2022, the direction finally reverted. All markets are inter-connected among themselves and with the economy.

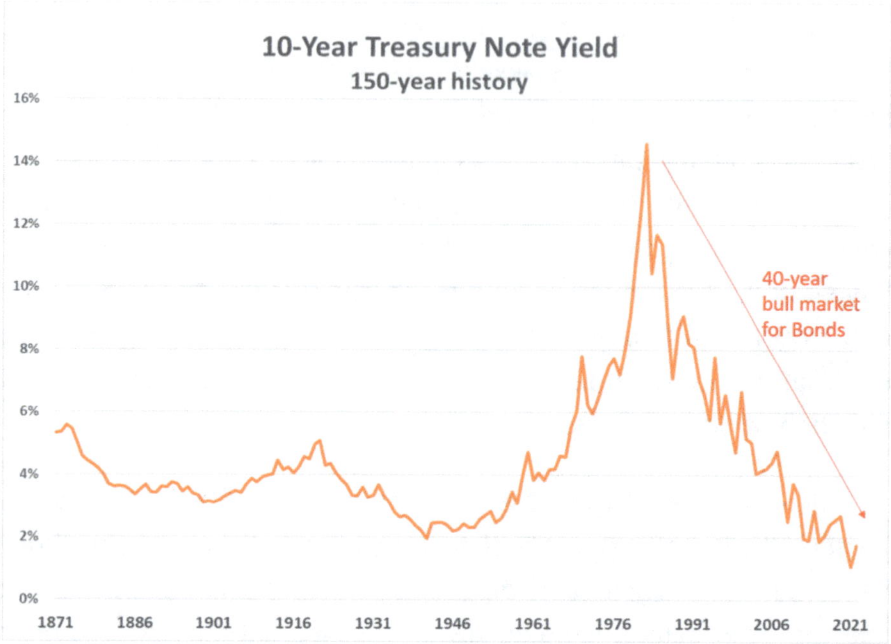

This is a perfect counterexample for those who believed bond risks are low. Bond risks are lower than stock risks, but they are not low. The Federal Reserve started hiking interest rates in 2022 to cool down the highest inflation in 40 years. This caused bond prices to tumble.

Interest rates are also important because they determine the pricing of all other assets in the economy. Interest rates determine the cost of money. Think about it. No one would leave large amounts of money simply sitting idle earning nothing, right? At the very minimum, they would invest in a savings account earning the minimum interest rate. Also, unless between family and friends, no one would lend money at zero interest rates. That is why interest rates work as a yardstick for all asset pricing in the rest of the economy.

But what determines interest rates? Ultimately, it is the Federal Reserve (Fed) through its monetary policy. In a nutshell, the Fed sets the benchmark Fed Funds rate, which is just an overnight lending rate for banks, at 8 Fed meetings scheduled throughout the year. Banks will balance their own accounts every night by borrowing from or lending to the Fed (or among themselves) at the Fed Funds rate. The projection for the trajectory of this very short rate into the future will determine the interest rates for the rest of tenors up to 30 years (tenor is the length of time for an investment). But the most important tenor widely used is the 10-year interest rate taken from the 10-year treasury note.

The Economy – Like markets, the economy also goes by cycles. Actually, if you think of the entire financial system as a big orchestra, the economy is the conductor, and the markets are the musicians. It's the economy that ultimately sets the rhythm of everything moving through the cycles. In a growing economy, all markets get on in an optimistic mode. In times of economic uncertainty, the markets tend to move sideways with wide swings (more volatile) as if they are confused and seeking direction. Therefore, keeping an eye on the economy, in addition to the markets, is very important. There are many key economic indicators that I watch daily, but for simplicity, I picked the 3 most important ones for a non-professional investor to keep track of: GDP growth rate, interest rates, and inflation rate.

- **GDP growth rate**: GDP (Gross Domestic Product) measures the level of economic activity. A positive and growing GDP growth rate quarter after quarter favors stock prices and real estate prices too, especially in locations with the highest growth in economic activity. A negative or declining GDP growth rate is bad for stock prices and bad for real estate prices. People's incomes suffer and typically downgrade, so residential multifamily investment properties see occupation levels suffer, along with rents. Of course, stocks pick the signal from changing economic prospects the fastest, and they are always the first to react, almost instantly. Real estate prices will eventually go along but with a much longer delay. Note in the chart below that GDP growth rates fluctuate and go through cycles as well. When the GDP growth rate goes negative for two consecutive quarters, economists call it a recession.

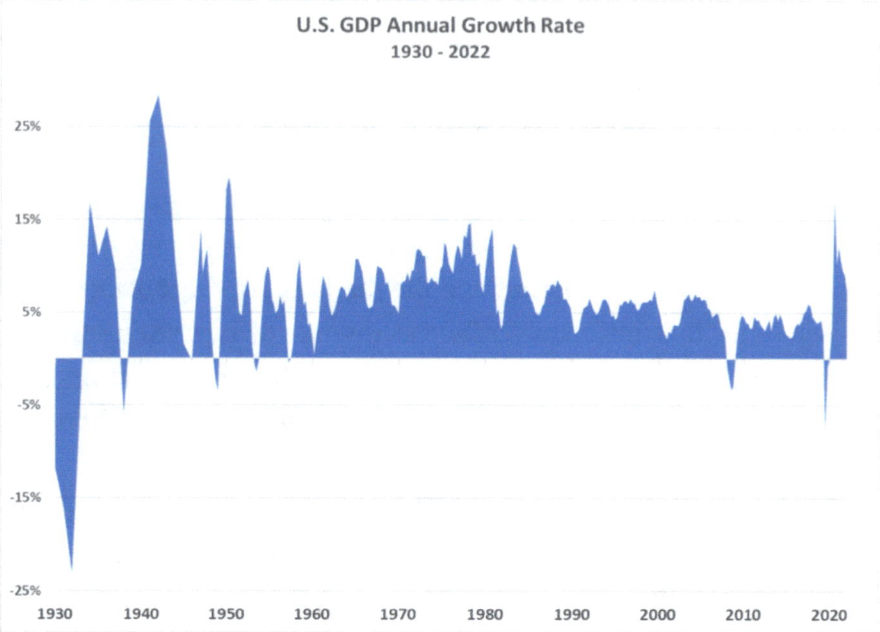

- **Interest rates**: High interest rates increase the cost of money in the economy and slow down the economy, reducing the GDP growth rate. This is bad for stock prices and real estate prices. In addition, higher interest rates will make mortgages more expensive, reducing home affordability and increasing pressure on housing prices. Conversely, low interest rates decrease the cost of money in the economy. That is why in the previous decade, people referred to "cheap money" fueling bubbles in asset prices. When interest rates are low, money flows to higher yielding assets like stocks and real estate.
- **Inflation rates**: Inflation erodes the purchasing power of money. The same dollar that once bought a cup of coffee no longer does; that's inflation. High inflation rates aren't good

for stocks. Moderate inflation is okay (by moderate, I mean, below 4-5%). Real estate can withstand effects of high inflation better than stocks. Rents can be readjusted for inflation every year. Low inflation rates benefit stocks and also real estate (lower costs of construction materials, etc.).

In summary, here is a cheat sheet for you for fast reference:

	Stocks	Real Estate
GDP growth rates	↑ = 👍 ↓ = 👎	↑ = 👍 ↓ = 👎
Interest rates	↑ = 👎 ↓ = 👍	↑ = 👎 ↓ = 👍
Inflation rates	↑ = 👎 ↓ = 👍	↑ = 👎 ↓ = 👍

Finally, to help you organize all the concepts into an easy, at-a-glance visualization of the picture of the current context, I created the tables below. You will be able to quickly assess the current situation and trends with them. I hope you will find them helpful when you make your decisions as to when to buy or sell assets, be those stocks or real estate, or any other type of asset, for that matter. They should also help you choose which assets to invest in, given the context.

Economic Fundamentals		
Interest rates	Inflation	Econ. growth
1-month view	6-month view	1-year view
Too high	Too high	On fire
Increasing	Increasing	Accelerating
Neutral	Neutral	Neutral
Decreasing	Decreasing	Decelerating
Too low	Too low	Recession

Real Estate Investing	
Prices	Rents
1-year view	1-year view
Emerging	Too high
Appreciating	Increasing
Turning point	Neutral
Depreciating	Decreasing
Recession	Too low

Stock Market Investing		
Current	Trend	Trend
For the day	1-month view	1-year view
Very Bullish	Very Bullish	Very Bullish
Bullish	Bullish	Bullish
Neutral	Neutral	Neutral
Bearish	Bearish	Bearish
Very Bearish	Very Bearish	Very Bearish

Fixed Rate Bond Investing		
Current	Trend	Trend
For the day	1-month view	1-year view
Very Bullish	Very Bullish	Very Bullish
Bullish	Bullish	Bullish
Neutral	Neutral	Neutral
Bearish	Bearish	Bearish
Very Bearish	Very Bearish	Very Bearish

(View as of January 10, 2023)

Before we wrap up this topic, I just want to mention that you may need to rotate your assets from time to time, such as selling underperforming assets and properties that will require higher repair costs soon, for example. There are many reasons you may want to get rid of some assets in exchange for new assets of the same (or different) type in your portfolio. And this can happen at any time. But try to time the execution of the sale and the purchase at a good time, whenever possible (sometimes it won't be possible and that's okay). I say good time because there is **no such thing as perfect timing**. Timing the peak and the bottom of a market cycle is virtually impossible. We may get close, and that is already good enough. Personally, I prefer to wait for the market to have already reverted to the direction I believe it will take because that could be a confirmation. I never take action before the reversion has already happened. This means past the peak or the bottom candidates. I call them candidates because the challenge is that you will never be sure if that was really the peak or the bottom because the market can always revert back to the original direction. Sometimes we will be right and sometimes we will be wrong. But the whole point of the 2nd principle of AFFF is not to be blind to the external context. Otherwise, it would be like walking with a blindfold.

"Timing the markets is impossible." – Is it? You must have heard this argument multiple times. Many pundits argue that timing the market is impossible. And the most commonly offered solution is just to ignore it completely by investing for the "long run." But for how long is left up to individual interpretation. How long is long enough (10 years, 20 years, 40 perhaps)? For example, look at the famous case of the Japanese stock market index, the Nikkei 225, which hasn't recovered its lost peak in over 30 years. Imagine an investor who bought his/her last Japanese stocks in 1989, waiting for the market to recover for them to sell for a profit. They would still be waiting today, after 33 years and counting because it is still nowhere near 38,000 points! Sorry, I don't buy this "long run" argument. I think we should not turn a blind eye to timing just because we can't time the market perfectly.

So, here is my point: facing something we can't do with perfection doesn't mean we shouldn't do it at all. I can't predict or be sure whether the market has bottomed or peaked yet, but still, I will study the market for clues and do my best. Stock traders are always working under uncertainty, trying to time the markets. And professional traders still manage to make a lot of money with imperfect tools and no crystal ball. Remember, you don't need to be perfect to be profitable. Did you know that the computer aboard Apollo 11, which landed on the Moon, had less computing power than the smartphone in your pocket? You really don't need to be perfect to accomplish great things. Forget perfection! You don't need perfect timing; you only need to be aware where in the cycle markets are at the present moment and to where the cycle is trending. Ask yourself where is the pendulum now and to where is it swinging? This is really not that hard. It's often in the news. In my humble opinion, ignoring what is going on around you is like walking blindfolded. And that is dangerous.

Incredibly, that's exactly what static rules of thumb are doing for you. By leaving your investments on autopilot, following a simplistic rule of thumb, unattended or watched by no one, you are actually ignoring what is going on around you. Are you not? Of course, a good and diligent advisor should keep your best interests at heart and alert you or act on your behalf; but again, you should be the boss in the driver's seat of this relationship. That is exactly what I think you should do if you are serious about reaching your financial freedom faster. You should be in charge. Advisors can really help you a great deal with their expertise, but you must be the ultimate decision maker. To do that effectively, you must be on top of what is going on around you. Remember, financial freedom is your goal, your personal target you have set for yourself to achieve. Embrace the role. Own it. No one else will be as focused on it as yourself.

Principle #3 – Borrow the strength of a greater force (Leverage with OPM)

You have already seen earlier when I introduced the AFFF that using OPM would shorten the travel distance to your so desired financial freedom. It would not only speed up the journey to arrive at your destination much sooner, but it will also require much less money from your own pocket. This is because, with OPM, you are not solely counting on your own financial power (earnings and savings) but also on the financial resources of a 3rd party, which is much more powerful than yours alone.

The most commonly known form of OPM is a mortgage loan in real estate. Banks are more than willing to lend you money at an LTV that varies from 50% to 80% (sometimes even higher) of your property's appraised value. LTV means "loan to value," which is simply the percentage of the property's appraised value the lender agrees to lend on. Lenders will send their own trusted professional appraisers to determine the value of your target property before acquisition.

Real estate is the most appropriate asset for lending due to a few important factors that financial assets typically don't possess. That is because the asset is taken as the collateral for the loan. What attributes are desirable for assets given as collateral? First, it must be a good storage of value. Second, its value should be stable and not too volatile. Third, it must have sure demand, so if the lender needs to take it to satisfy the unpaid loan balance, they can easily sell it to someone else to convert to cash. So, why is real estate such a good asset class for asset-based lending? It fits the bill for all 3 criteria. First, real estate is a real asset in the physical world. It is a good storage of value. Even if the building can deteriorate, the land the property sits upon will always have its intrinsic value. Second, real estate values don't move very fast, and they are relatively stable. Third, in general, most real estate properties will have demand, at the right price. That's why there is a mortgage industry.

The OPM/E - I call this type of OPM, leveraging real estate income-producing properties, OPM/E. The E stands for External, meaning it comes from external sources (because it is someone else's property yet to be acquired).

How about a portfolio of stocks and bonds as collateral? Financial assets usually don't fare very well with the 3 criteria, especially the second one. Values of stocks and bonds are just too volatile to be used as collateral. However, there are some private banks that offer loans for their wealthy clients based on the value of the portfolio the same bank manages on their behalf. This is an arrangement that fits the bank's interests because they usually charge high fees and commissions; while the client is indebted, the client will stay in the arrangement. If the value of the portfolio drops too much, they may require additional security. But in any event, unlike real estate assets, stocks and bonds are not very good as collateral, especially stocks.

When you buy a small business, you may also borrow from a loan secured by your business assets as collateral (equipment, etc.). It can be a bank loan guaranteed by the SBA (Small Business Administration), or it can also be a seller-finance transaction associated with the purchase.

Besides real estate mortgages and secure business loans, there is another little-known asset that closely fits the criteria to be a collateral. You may have, but I suspect you probably have not, heard of policy loans from life insurance companies. I always thought life insurance was just that: insurance to ensure that the descendants of the breadwinner of a family will be taken care of financially should he/she pass away too early. I thought that a life insurance policy worked like any other type of insurance (e.g., car insurance, health insurance, etc.): you pay premiums every month, and should a specified event happen (a car accident or theft for car insurance, a sickness for health insurance, or death for life insurance), you will receive money from the insurance company to cover your expenses or a fixed amount, like the death benefit. But I had never seen life insurance as an asset!

Life insurance is actually an asset, I later learned. Think about it. You make a series of payments (premium) in exchange for larger payments back at future dates. It looks a lot like an investment in terms of the cash flow (except that it is subject upon the occurrence of a specified event). But not all insurance policies are assets that can be used as collateral. For example, term life insurance policies are never accepted as collateral. Term life does not have something called cash value. But whole life and universal life do. Universal life has a problem, though. It's often based on the stock market, so its cash value can fluctuate. Unlike universal life, whole life is the best asset for asset-based lending. The guaranteed portion of whole life's cash value grows like a fixed income investment. It's highly stable and predictable. The insurance company even guarantees the fixed growth rate (the guaranteed portion of cash value). Since the insurance company holds the asset, it can easily lend money to you holding the cash value as collateral.

The OPM/I - I call this OPM/I, in which I stands for Internal. This is because the source is from an insurance policy you already own, therefore it's a collateral based on your own internal sources. For more information about how the entire thing works, please follow the instructions in Chapter 9.

These three modes of OPM – mortgage loans, business loans, and whole life policy loans – are the main types you can use for the 3rd principle of AFFF. They work as boosters to accelerate your journey to financial freedom. In the diagram below you can see their similarities and differences.

OPM/E vs. OPM/I

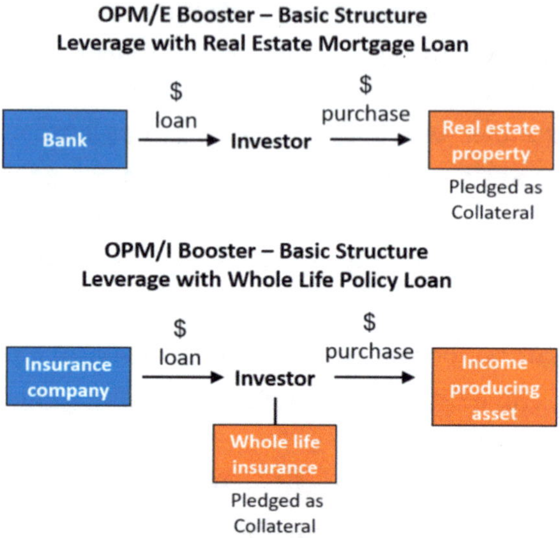

Important note: While OPM/E (leveraged real estate with a mortgage) accelerates your journey to financial freedom by lowering your Target Capital, OPM/I is not going to help much at the beginning of your journey, unless you already own whole life policies with cash value. Assuming you don't, you have to start a new policy and start funding your policy via premiums first. This may take a few years. OPM/I starts to exhibit its power after you have a chance to accumulate a substantial amount of cash value inside your policy. The premiums you pay to fund your policy will build up cash value. The good news is that there are ways to speed up cash value buildup! The policy must be designed expertly by a knowledgeable structurer with that end in mind. Once you have sufficient cash value built up, the insurance company will typically lend you up to 95% of the amount of the cash value. Unlike a mortgage, you won't need to qualify for the loan. Yes, you heard me right. No need to prove income. No credit scores or reports required. You are always approved because the collateral is already controlled by the insurance company, which is your own cash value in the policy. Therefore, you may be sure you can always get the loan. After you take the loan, you can invest in anything you want, but under the AFFF framework, I'd suggest you invest in an income-producing asset like a real estate property.

And it gets better than that. The interest rate is often lower than mortgage rates. If you miss a mortgage payment, you will receive an unpleasant delinquency notice. If you still don't pay, the bank will foreclose on your property, and you may lose your property entirely. But you won't ever have this problem with a whole life policy loan. In other words, there are simply no fixed repayment schedules. You can pay the insurance company back at any time you choose and the amount you choose. What? Yes, you heard me right. It's an unstructured loan, which means there are really no terms for repayment. That's right, I said no income check, no credit check, and you can repay any way you want and when you want. I know it sounds too good to be true. Well, it's easy to explain why with an extreme example. Suppose you took the loan and never paid back. This means that you passed away without ever returning the money you borrowed. What happens is that after you pass away, the insurance company must pay a sizeable amount of death benefit to your beneficiaries. At this moment, the insurance company will simply deduct your balance due (principal plus interest) from the death benefit and pay the remainder to your designated beneficiaries. Does it make sense now?

Notice that while term life insurance does nothing for the insured while he/she is alive (it only benefits their heirs at death), whole life insurance can be used to provide funding for the insured's investments during his/her lifetime. For you as an investor, this is a lot of power to plan the financing of your investment projects. You have more control with OPM/I than OPM/E.

Since OPM/I is an insurance policy, let's not forget the death benefit, which is usually a relatively big amount, to be paid to your beneficiaries. This is great for estate planning and wealth transfer to your next generation. For a financial freedom seeker who got that far, I call that stage **Full Financial Freedom**. Most financial freedom proponents stop much earlier, which is when passive income from investments is just enough to pay for the person's lifestyle expense. This is what I call **Basic Financial Freedom**. Now you can see the value of the AFFF. It proposes to take you much farther than other financial freedom proponents.

The whole life insurance cash value can also supplement your income

Besides providing OPM/I to boost our investments and a death benefit to our loved ones when we depart from this world, a whole life policy can do a lot more for us. For example, the cash value itself in your policy can be used as income. You can make regular withdrawals at any time. This money can replace income from other sources during your retirement, if necessary. Therefore, it adds security to your retirement income needs. Since you have the control, you decide how much you withdraw because, remember, the more you withdraw, the less money you'd be leaving to your beneficiaries after you pass. Here is an example:

Stacey is a 38-year-old woman who bought a whole life insurance policy and designated her 5-year-old son, Bobby, as the beneficiary. She selected a "Paid up at 65" whole life policy, designed to be funded by the time she reaches age 65. She agreed to pay $18,000 annual premiums until that age, by which the policy will be deemed paid up and no more premiums will be required. This would give her an immediate death benefit of $898,162 when she starts her policy should she pass away. Before you scream, "Oh, I can't afford paying $18,000 annual premiums," note that this is just an example. A competent life insurance designer should be able to structure a policy tailor-made to your specific needs and circumstances. Each policy should be different. Check out Stacey's policy illustration below, projecting her future cashflow, assuming she will live until age 85 and leave the death benefit to Bobby. Note the 3 distinct phases over this long-term plan:

Year	Age	Cashflow	Cash Value	D. Benefit
1	39	-18,000	2,473	898,162
2	40	-18,000	7,404	907,231
3	41	-18,000	24,751	916,635
4	42	-18,000	42,785	926,426
5	43	-18,000	61,520	936,597
6	44	-18,000	81,095	947,388
7	45	-18,000	101,549	958,869
8	46	-18,000	122,921	971,022
9	47	-18,000	145,251	983,971
10	48	-18,000	168,567	997,673
11	49	-18,000	193,001	1,012,381
12	50	-18,000	218,602	1,028,075
13	51	-18,000	245,416	1,044,766
14	52	-18,000	273,540	1,062,572
15	53	-18,000	303,056	1,081,511
16	54	-18,000	334,261	1,102,207
17	55	-18,000	367,141	1,124,412
18	56	-18,000	401,769	1,148,133
19	57	-18,000	438,236	1,173,374
20	58	-18,000	476,621	1,200,151
21	59	-18,000	517,140	1,230,473
22	60	-18,000	560,739	1,264,300
23	61	-18,000	607,535	1,301,603
24	62	-18,000	657,721	1,342,427
25	63	-18,000	711,421	1,386,720
26	64	-18,000	768,852	1,434,555
27	65	-18,000	830,173	1,485,927
28	66	50,000	821,634	1,437,001
29	67	50,000	812,602	1,389,182
30	68	50,000	803,051	1,342,401
31	69	50,000	792,948	1,296,599
32	70	50,000	782,298	1,251,737
33	71	50,000	771,037	1,207,690
34	72	50,000	759,117	1,164,380
35	73	50,000	746,513	1,121,716
36	74	50,000	733,187	1,079,629
37	75	50,000	719,063	1,044,551
38	76	50,000	704,060	1,025,037
39	77	50,000	688,087	1,003,990
40	78	50,000	671,039	981,315
41	79	50,000	652,610	956,632
42	80	50,000	632,827	930,000
43	81	50,000	611,489	901,246
44	82	50,000	588,436	870,308
45	83	50,000	563,591	837,193
46	84	50,000	536,795	801,778
47	85	50,000	**507,822**	**763,917**

- **The funding phase (age 39 to 65):** Stacey funded $18,000 annually to her policy, totaling $486,000 injected over 27 years.
- **The distribution phase (age 66 to 85):** Stacey will withdraw $50,000 annually from her policy, totaling $1,000,000 over 20 years.
- **The final legacy phase (the last year):** Bobby will receive the death benefit in the amount of $763,917 upon Stacey's passing.

What if Stacey also has other investments as additional sources of income and she decides to withdrawal less money from her whole life policy? Let's assume she decided to take $40,000 a year instead of $50,000 and see how the numbers would change:

Year	Age	Cashflow	Cash Value	D. Benefit
1	39	-18,000	2,473	898,162
2	40	-18,000	7,404	907,231
3	41	-18,000	24,751	916,635
4	42	-18,000	42,785	926,426
5	43	-18,000	61,520	936,597
6	44	-18,000	81,095	947,388
7	45	-18,000	101,549	958,869
8	46	-18,000	122,921	971,022
9	47	-18,000	145,251	983,971
10	48	-18,000	168,567	997,673
11	49	-18,000	193,001	1,012,381
12	50	-18,000	218,602	1,028,075
13	51	-18,000	245,416	1,044,766
14	52	-18,000	273,540	1,062,572
15	53	-18,000	303,056	1,081,511
16	54	-18,000	334,261	1,102,207
17	55	-18,000	367,141	1,124,412
18	56	-18,000	401,769	1,148,133
19	57	-18,000	438,236	1,173,374
20	58	-18,000	476,621	1,200,151
21	59	-18,000	517,140	1,230,473
22	60	-18,000	560,739	1,264,300
23	61	-18,000	607,535	1,301,603
24	62	-18,000	657,721	1,342,427
25	63	-18,000	711,421	1,386,720
26	64	-18,000	768,852	1,434,555
27	65	-18,000	830,173	1,485,927
28	66	40,000	832,147	1,455,388
29	67	40,000	834,164	1,426,044
30	68	40,000	836,223	1,397,853
31	69	40,000	838,316	1,370,784
32	70	40,000	840,476	1,344,826
33	71	40,000	842,661	1,319,876
34	72	40,000	844,848	1,295,878
35	73	40,000	847,036	1,272,763
36	74	40,000	849,212	1,250,478
37	75	40,000	851,329	1,228,966
38	76	40,000	853,379	1,208,188
39	77	40,000	855,341	1,188,122
40	78	40,000	857,116	1,181,635
41	79	40,000	858,432	1,176,370
42	80	40,000	859,357	1,170,093
43	81	40,000	859,731	1,162,672
44	82	40,000	859,439	1,154,096
45	83	40,000	858,459	1,144,433
46	84	40,000	856,683	1,133,609
47	85	40,000	**853,936**	**1,121,535**

- **The funding phase (age 39 to 65):** Stacey funded $18,000 annually to her policy, totaling $486,000 injected over 27 years. No change here.
- **The distribution phase (age 66 to 85):** Stacey will withdraw $40,000 annually from her policy, totaling $800,000 over 20 years.
- **The final legacy phase (the last year):** Bobby will receive the death benefit in the amount of $1,121,535 upon Stacey's passing.

Note that the control is in Stacey's hands. She decides whether she wants to withdraw every year and how much. If she withdraws less, she leaves more to Bobby, and vice-versa. This flexibility as an alternative income source for those on the road to financial freedom, who invariably will be investing in other assets at the same time, provides more security and stability for their entire journey.

For example, assume Stacey's income needs are fully satisfied by her investments made under the AFFF framework so she doesn't need to withdraw any money from her whole life policy. That way, she would leave the maximum death benefit to Bobby. But let's say that in a certain year, she encounters serious headwinds in her investments. For example, a multi-family building generating a large portion of her income got struck by a natural disaster not covered by insurance, which caused a serious reduction to her income. Thankfully, she has this whole life policy with enough cash value so she can take withdrawals. But as soon as the problem is resolved and her income from the multi-family building is resumed, she can stop taking money from her whole life policy and leave more to Bobby in the future. This example illustrated for you that a whole life policy:

- Can be used as an emergency fund for unexpected cash needs.
- Offers flexibility to provide more stability and predictability to a financial plan.
- Gives the policyowner the power to decide how to best allocate the funds in the policy.

There are incredible tax advantages here, too, if the policy is properly designed. But the point I want to make is that this feature adds stability and safety to your financial journey to Full Financial Freedom.

Quick note: There are two ways to access the cash value in a whole life policy: withdrawals and loans. In Stacey's example, she took withdrawals. I believe loans are generally more advantageous. With loans, your cash value remains intact and continues earning interest. There are also tax advantages, as loans aren't taxable as income. The impact of loans and withdrawals on cash value and death benefit will also be different. Be sure to request an illustration from the insurance company's customer service illustrating both scenarios to help you decide which is the most advantageous to your situation.

Before we wrap up this topic, remember I said OPM/I might not help you very much in terms of speed in the early years of your journey (assuming you have no whole life policy and would have to start a new one). The beauty of OPM/I is that it will help you tremendously in the mid and final sections of your journey to give stability, safety, and acceleration to Full Financial Freedom.

For all the above reasons, both the OPM/E and OPM/I qualify as boosters to any serious financial freedom plan, specifically, the AFFF. They work behind the scenes and rarely get the attention they deserve. Everyone likes to think and talk about investment A, B, or C, and rates of return. Rarely do you hear of someone digging deeper to take advantage of the inner mechanisms of how money really works. But these boosters help you save money and bring the target closer to you. This is how OPM /E and /I can accelerate your journey to financial freedom.

Principle #4 – Money Boosters (Optimization of Money)

This is a key topic that everyone should understand when planning their finances, but strangely it is often neglected by traditional financial freedom methods. Even renowned finance authors don't cover it to any extent. But I will not only provide you with an introduction right now in this book, but also publish a separate book entirely dedicated to this subject. The book will be part of the AFFF Collection Series and be titled *Money Boosters*. You can also learn more in Chapter 9 and how to get find additional information in Chapter 11. Knowing how money works and how to minimize money leaks (money that we inadvertently let escape through our fingers) can seriously accelerate your journey to financial freedom and wealth buildup. This is exactly the 4th principle of the AFFF. It also covers several other foundation issues with money. The 4th principle of the AFFF encompasses the following super-important concepts, making the 8 pillars of the Money Boosters strategy:

1. The Time Value of Money: often neglected in favor of higher returns, time can be just as powerful.
2. The Magic of Compound Interest.
3. The Real Cost of Interrupting Compound Interest.
4. The Lost Opportunity Cost: you finance everything you buy. Even cash has a cost.
5. The 10 Wealth Eroding Factors. Procrastination itself is one: every day counts.
6. Fix your Money Leaks even before you think about saving money.
7. Focus on Volume of Interest, instead of Interest Rates.
8. Borrow Other People's Money to Invest: pay interest on a declining principal (by amortization) and earn interest on an increasing principal (by compounding interest).

Because the material is very extensive for this book, I will provide a brief introduction here and a 30,000-foot broad view of a few of the above 8 pillars. I strongly suggest you learn the details in the Module 1- *Accelerate with* OPM/I Money Boosters (directions in Chapter 9 or Chapter 11).

1. The Time Value of Money: often neglected in favor of higher returns, time can be just as powerful

What is the investor's most important formula? It is the future value for an investment made today, isn't it? Let's take another close look at it:

$$\textbf{\textit{Future Value}} = \textbf{\textit{Present Value}} \times (\mathbf{1} + \textbf{\textit{Return Rate}})^{\textbf{\textit{Time}}}$$

As investors, we look at the above formula, and what do we do? We only see Present Value (the higher the amount we invest, the larger the amount of money we make) and Rate of Return (the higher the rate of return, the larger the amount of money we make). But what about that little, almost imperceptible variable in the exponent, called Time? It is often neglected, isn't it? It is right in front of us all the time, but we tend to focus on the other two variables. We assume time is a given and it is the same for everyone. Therefore, it should not be a differentiation factor. Incredibly, we are wrong.

Most of us are so focused on maximizing our rates of return that we often ignore the T I M E factor. We are always chasing rates of return, are we not? We want to buy stocks with the greatest potential to grow, bonds with the highest yields, and investment properties that yield the highest cashflow for the amount invested. It's natural, nothing wrong with it. But there is always the other side of the coin that's unavoidable: higher returns mean higher risks as well. The pair is inseparable. That's why there's a limit to the returns we should desire. We can chase higher rates of return as much as we want, but there is a limit, or we will end up taking unacceptable risks with which we aren't comfortable.

But TIME doesn't have this problem. Time doesn't come attached to risks the same way rates of return do. Time is universal to all. Time is also the most valuable asset we all share.

How can you explore the time factor? The first and most straightforward answer is – start investing early – as early as possible. The biggest problem is that people procrastinate. "Oh, I don't know what to invest in," and they delay taking any action and time is wasted. If you have this problem, I have the perfect antidote for you: seek financial education. As soon as possible. I offer courses from basic to advanced and also a mentorship program if you need. Check out my author website, if you haven't already. There are other sources of education out there too, but just make sure they are from a reputable and experienced person. Preferably, someone with credentials. These days, overnight experts are popping out everywhere on the internet and YouTube.

If possible, keep money invested at all times. The longer your money is working for you, the greater the amount of return you are going to get from it. Keep your money working for you 365 days a year, 7 days a week, and 24 hours a day. These are basic concepts, and most people already know them in essence: invest early, invest often, and keep invested longer.

2. The Magic of Compound Interest

$1 doubling 20 times

Day	Amount
0	1.00
1	2.00
2	4.00
3	8.00
4	16.00
5	32.00
6	64.00
7	128.00
8	256.00
9	512.00
10	1,024.00
11	2,048.00
12	4,096.00
13	8,192.00
14	16,384.00
15	32,768.00
16	65,536.00
17	131,072.00
18	262,144.00
19	524,288.00
20	**1,048,576.00**

Simply put, compound interest is merely reinvestment. You reinvest interest earned in one period into the next period of time. In other words, the interest you've just earned becomes additional principal. You can see where this game, repeated over and over, will take you. Think of a snowball rolling downhill. As it rolls, it accretes more and more snow, growing bigger and bigger. This is exactly what you want for your money! But the key point for your financial freedom acceleration feature can be seen now: note that just like in the snowball analogy, the speed of the snow accretion, or money accumulation, increases over time. Speed increase over time has a name in physics: acceleration.

Here is an extreme example to magnify the effect of compound interest so you can see it more clearly. Imagine you have an oversized rate of return of 100% a day. Your money will double every day. I know it's absurd, but it will help you see more clearly. Let's start with $1.00 (one dollar). How much money would we have in 20 days? $1,048,576.00. That is the power of compound interest. The earnings from one period become additional principal for the next period. Earnings are re-invested. Now back to the real world. Even with much lower rates of return, it is exactly the same principle. The math is the same.

The compound interest (or snowballing) effect only works if you keep money invested. It is so obvious, but do we do this all the time? This is the subject of the next pillar.

3. The Real Cost of Interrupting Compound Interest

Do you know something we all do in our daily lives, mostly unknowingly or by giving it no thought, which makes us bleed money and with it our financial future? We are actually doing it all the time by taking withdrawals from our investments. Of course, life goes on and we need money for so many things in life. We sell assets, withdraw money from savings, redeem shares from funds, don't we? We spend the cash for our living expenses, some big events (wedding, college, purchase of a car, a house, etc.). This is life and it is totally fine. However, we must be aware that there is a cost associated with it: you break the magic of compound interest. In other words, by selling assets or withdrawing money from investments that earn you money, you interrupted the intrinsic compound interest mechanism in these investments.

$1 doubling 20 times

Day	Amount
0	1.00
1	2.00
2	4.00
3	8.00
4	16.00
5	32.00
6	64.00
7	128.00
8	256.00
9	512.00
10	1,024.00
11	2,048.00
12	4,096.00
13	8,192.00
14	16,384.00
15	32,768.00
16	1.00
17	2.00
18	4.00
19	8.00
20	**16.00**

Can we use the same example above to show this to you? Let's say that after the balance of your investment of $1.00 doubling every day reached $32,768.00, on the 15th day, you decided to withdraw the money accumulated in that incredible investment account. "Well," you thought, "I can always put money back and start this incredible investment over, can't I?" This is correct. You restart with $1 on the 16th day. However, look what happened to your account on the 20th day: your new balance will be just $16.00. **Hey, where did the $1 million go?**

One million dollars evaporated. Because you interrupted the compound interest effect, you killed a million dollars from future existence. That is the cost of interrupting compound interest. In this example, it just cost you $1 million in your future.

Of course, this is an extreme example, but again, the principle is exactly the same in our day-to-day personal finances. We must be mindful because dimes and nickels do add up over time, and we may be missing fortunes over time.

Missed Fortunes: Why is everyone not a millionaire by the time they retire?

Baby Boomers savings, by percentages	
Less than $50,000	37%
Between $50,000 and $100,000	13%
Between $100,000 and $200,000	14%
Between $200,000 and $300,000	12%
Between $300,000 and $500,000	9%
Over $500,000	15%

Data source: PWC Employee Financial Wellness Survey

This is truly a sad statistic. How much savings do baby boomers have in their retirement accounts by their retirement ages around 65? While some experts and TV celebrity pundits contend that a person needs at least $5 million in his/her retirement account by age 65 to ensure a comfortable and secure retirement, this is by far not the reality for the vast majority of our seniors. See in the table that 85% of baby boomers retiring nowadays had less than $500,000, and 50% had less than $100,000. *That* is the sad reality. While the $5 million figure may be up to debate, we don't need any sophisticated model or expert to tell us that $100,000 is obviously insufficient and even $500,000 may not be enough for a comfortable and stress-free retirement. People are living longer.

The decisions we make today will result in what future reality we will find ourselves in. Do you want the $100,000 or $5,000,000 future reality? That will depend on choices you make today. We shape our future realities by decisions we make today. The investor's formula helps us understand it. The time factor is absolutely critical. Don't waste time. Keep your hard-earned dollars working for you 24/7/365.

Avoid interrupting compound earnings. Again, your future depends on the choices you make today.

The next five pillars will be covered in detail in my next book *Money Boosters* in the AFFF Collection Series (You may also check out the contents ahead of its publication in video: information in Chapter 11):

4. **The Lost Opportunity Cost: you finance everything you buy. Even cash has a cost.**
5. **The 10 Wealth Eroding Factors. Procrastination itself is one: every day counts.**
6. **Fix Your Money Leaks even before you think about saving money.**
7. **Focus on Volume of Interest, instead of Interest Rates.**
8. **Borrow Other People's Money to Invest: Pay interest on a declining principal (by amortization) and earn interest on an increasing principal (by compounding interest).**

I'm sure these concepts are rather unique if fully employed in a financial freedom plan. They will be thoroughly explained in the *Money Boosters* book (see directions in Chapter 9). **Pillar #8** is particularly fantastic: you can have your money working double duty or working in two places at the same time for you. Let me give you a quick spoiler.

Pillar #8 can be better accomplished with a whole life insurance instrument. Let's recap how whole life insurance works. You make periodic payments (premiums) to fund an investment account called "cash value." The account balance will be invested by the insurance company in various markets, and the earnings obtained from these investments will grow the account (cash value). As investors, we are more interested in the cash value growth than the death benefit, initially. One of the best things that can be accomplished with whole life is to structure in a way that it can grow tax free, but that is a discussion I will leave for the *Money Boosters* book. For now, I will focus on the use of policy loans to fund asset purchases, such as an income-producing asset like real estate.

OPM/I Booster – Basic Structure
Leverage with Whole Life Policy Loan

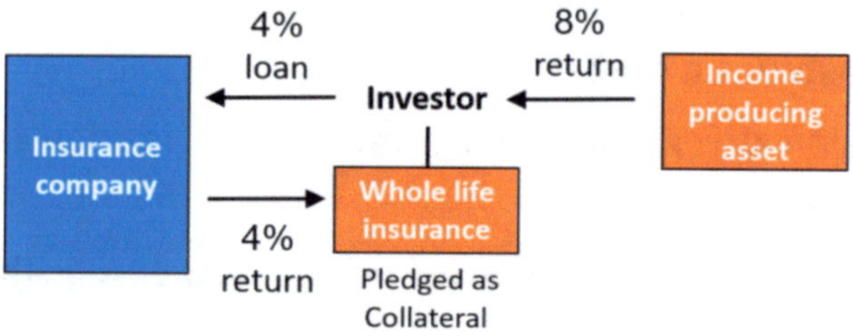

Look at the diagram. Let's say I took a policy loan at 4% based on my whole life policy's cash value. This borrowed money will be used to buy an income-producing asset like real estate, returning me a cashflow yield of 8% (also called cap rate). That is OPM/I, and it is great that a 4% loan is leveraging an 8% return asset. So far so good.

But remember that my cash value itself inside the policy is also growing near 4%. Normally, the loan rate and the cash value growth rate of a fully funded whole life policy are pretty similar. So, here is where most people get it wrong. They think that the 4% loan rate and the 4% cash value growth are a wash. One cancels out the other, so why bother? Well, that thinking is not exactly right. The secret is how you do it. Here is the secret recipe:

On the loan side, make payments over a declining balance (amortize it).

On the investment side, receive earnings over a growing balance (compound it).

LOAN SIDE

Rate	6%
Tenor	60
Amount	100,000
PMT	1,933

Month	Beg. Bal.	Payment	Interest	Amortiz.	End Bal.
1	100,000	1,933	500	1,433	98,567
2	98,567	1,933	493	1,440	97,126
3	97,126	1,933	486	1,448	95,679
4	95,679	1,933	478	1,455	94,224
5	94,224	1,933	471	1,462	92,762
6	92,762	1,933	464	1,469	91,292
	(...)				
57	7,637	1,933	38	1,895	5,742
58	5,742	1,933	29	1,905	3,838
59	3,838	1,933	19	1,914	1,924
60	1,924	1,933	10	1,924	(0)
	Total	**115,997**	**15,997**		

INVESTMENT SIDE

Rate	4%
Tenor	60
Amoun	100,000

Month	Beg. Bal.	Interest	End Bal.
1	100,000	333	100,333
2	100,333	334	100,668
3	100,668	336	101,003
4	101,003	337	101,340
5	101,340	338	101,678
6	101,678	339	102,017
	(...)		
57	120,485	402	120,887
58	120,887	403	121,290
59	121,290	404	121,694
60	121,694	406	**122,100**
	Total	**22,100**	

How powerful is the above procedure? Let me answer with a numerical example for easier understanding. How about borrowing at 6% and investing at 4%? I bet the vast majority of people will say this is a certain losing proposition. Yes, but that is only true if you earn interest and pay interest the same way. If we pay interest over a declining balance but earn interest over an expanding balance, we may still turn out profitable borrowing at 6% and investing at 4%. Doubt it? Let me show you the math:

On the loan side, I repaid my 6%, 60-month, $100,000 loan on an amortizing schedule. After 60 months, paying $1,933 per month, I paid off the loan. The total amount of interest paid was $15,997.

On the investment side, my balance grew at 4% on a compound interest regime. After 60 months, the total amount of earnings collected was $22,100.

So, there you have an example of how investing at a lower rate than borrowing can still be profitable. But in reality, you will probably never need to do such a thing; it was just an example to show you the power of the strategy. In a reputable life insurance company, the loan rate will be similar to the cash value's growth rate of a fully funded policy. If you use this in your AFFF plan, you will see how it will help boost the speed of your journey to financial freedom.

You are already seeing the power in understanding how money works so you can work smarter. This is how you make more money without taking up any additional risk. It can be accomplished just by changing the way you do things you already do (change the method).

Interestingly, I don't see other authors talking about these things incorporated in their financial freedom plans. All these concepts working together are powerful to give more bang for your hard-earned buck and will help you accelerate your journey to financial freedom.

The real advantage of the Accelerated Financial Freedom Formula™

What sets it apart from Traditional methods

To wrap up this chapter, let's summarize the AFFF and compare it again side-by-side with mainstream traditional methods. In stark contrast to these methods, the AFFF method will use a multi-asset approach (real estate, financial markets, insurance, and small business) on a context-dependent tactical allocation method (just a fancy way to say that investment decisions will depend on the economy and markets). The multidimensionality of the AFFF will give you more choices. Even if all markets are bad at the same time, there will still be some better than others, whether you are entering or exiting. Choice is power! The context dependency will make it a dynamic strategy (it changes with the changes in the economy and markets) in stark contrast to static strategies preached by mainstream traditional methods. Plus, the AFFF will gain another serious push by booster accelerators (OPM or leverage) and money optimization techniques (the AFFF also thrives on compound earnings, strives to stop or minimize money leaks – money that escapes through our fingers, often invisibly, without us even noticing – and recovers lost opportunity costs.) Here is a summary to show you at a glance how AFFF is so different from traditional methods out there for financial freedom and retirement planning:

Major Differences	The AFFF	Traditional methods
Asset types employed	Multi-asset types: • Real estate + • Stocks & bonds + • Life insurance as OPM/I + • Autorun small business	Generally, single-asset type: • Real estate only; or • Stocks & bonds only.
Context-dependent	Yes, including asset selection and allocation, timing the markets	Generally, no Follows a static strategy or rule
Use of OPM / leverage	Yes, with real estate (mortgage) and financial / whole life insurance (policy loans)	Real estate: generally, yes. Financial: generally, no.
Money Boosters (Optimized use of money)	Yes, learn how to identify and stop money leaks, recover lost opportunity costs, and use money with maximum efficiency	Not even addressed
Acceleration	Yes: • Capital formation speed up • Capital target lowered down • Max money efficiency	No, too dependent on markets: • Capital formation: little control • Capital target: static, fixed and way too high of a target for most people to reach
Go beyond financial freedom	Yes, it addresses legacy to protect descendants, adds income stability, and ways to protect your wealth	Rarely addressed

CHAPTER 6

6. Why the AFFF works - The mathematical proof

Normally, at this point, another author might just provide a long list of testimonials to show how a method worked for a lot of people. This is great. I don't know about you, but I'm not easily convinced just because of other people's testimonials; I require deeper proof (right or wrong, that's just me). Therefore, I'm not going to do that. I shall instead provide you with a stronger kind of proof.

I do know for a fact that millions of people around the world have achieved financial freedom one way or another. Most of them used a single asset approach (typically either real estate or financial assets). You don't need to be a genius to understand that a multi-asset approach couldn't be any less effective than a single asset approach, because the latter is a just sub-set of the former. There is no logical reason for a multi-asset approach not to be superior to a single-asset approach.

Seeing is believing. This is universal. That's why I want to show you the numbers. I'm making all the numbers available for you in the Appendix. In addition, you may have a copy of my Excel sheets. To get a free copy of my Excel sheets, which you can use to simulate your own personal situation, just go to my author website at www.acceleratedfinancialfreedom.com to register and get access to these Excel sheets plus all downloadable files I make available for you now and in the future. Another advantage of registering at my website is that you will also receive a newsletter and future revisions of the book, new chapters with additions and improvements, free of charge. Find more information in Chapter 11.

What's truth? What kinds of truth exist? Maybe you know, maybe you don't, but in philosophy, there are 4 types of truth. I extracted these definitions from the HSD Institute's website:

- **Objective Truth** is what exists and can be proved in this physicality. (The sun moves across the sky each day.)
- **Normative Truth** is what we, as a group, agree is true. (English speakers agreed to use the word "day" to name that time when the sky is lit by the sun.)
- **Subjective Truth** is how the individual sees or experiences the world. (Today is a good day for me.)
- **Complex Truth** recognizes the validity of all those truths and allows you to focus on the one most useful at any given time. (The sun is up; the day is bright. Today is a good day for MOM, so let's take advantage of that and ask for ice cream for dinner.)

The reason I inserted this excerpt in the book is that I think it's important for us to put things into the right perspective. In the age of the internet and social media, all gurus and experts persuade their audiences by offering testimonials. In marketing, this is called "social proof." We humans are always seeking "social proof" to help us make decisions in subjects we are not very proficient to make our own judgments and we don't know the person trying to convince us of something. It's a shortcut for our brains to convince ourselves whether to trust in something or someone. Before making a purchase, we like to read testimonials and reviews from past customers. This is a good practice, and like everyone else, I do it myself. However, testimonials come from customers' personal experiences, also called anecdotal evidence. That's why opinions vary greatly. If you look at book reviews on Amazon, you will almost always see good and bad reviews sitting side by side. It's rarely universal; people do have different views, experiences, and assessments on the same object, be it a book, a movie, or a method. Reviews tend to be more reliable than testimonials because you can see the good and the bad; with testimonials you only see the good ones. If you choose to believe in reviews and testimonials as truth, you need to know these are what philosophers classify as **subjective truths**.

There is nothing wrong with subjective truths. But there are stronger forms of truths, like objective truths. A mathematical proof is an **objective truth**. For this reason, I prefer to offer you a **mathematical proof** in place of a long list of testimonials. I just think it's much stronger and holds the proof to a higher standard. Of course, when dealing with math, we make sure to carefully list the important assumptions we are making because models of reality are just approximations of reality. The proofs I'm presenting in the book do have assumptions about interest rates, return rates, LTV, etc., just like the rest of Wall Street practitioners and investment companies. But the soundness of the mathematical relationships is what really matters for what I'm trying to prove to you.

I showed you the basic framework of the AFFF. Once you understood its basic idea (speeding up capital formation and use of OPM to shorten the journey) and the 4 principles of AFFF (multi-asset, choosing assets strategically and in response to the external environment, leverage with OPM, and optimization of the use of money), the mechanism and why it works should become obvious to you, regardless of any numbers.

If you shorten the travel distance and/or run faster, you will arrive at the destination faster.

This is pure logic: **if you shorten the travel distance and/or run faster, you will arrive at the destination faster.** Won't you?

Having a choice is always superior, or at least the same, to having no choice.

And what about: **having a choice [from multiple assets to invest] is always superior, or at least the same, to having no choice**. Aren't these statements logically sound? I don't need to put numbers down to convince you about these two statements, and I also don't need 1,000 testimonials to convince you of them. Do I? This is objective truth. Also a logical proof, which should be even more powerful. And they are the foundation of the AFFF, as you already know.

Mathematicians can derive formulas upon formulas without a single number, just equations; that is objective truth if the logic is sound and mathematical rules are respected. However, mathematical proofs can be challenging for those not mathematically inclined; therefore, I decided to provide numbers (and formulas in Excel) instead of equations to help you understand the method. I will give you my spreadsheet called **The Flightplan Simulator**. In it, there are no hidden cells or formulas. You can audit all the formulas and see how calculations are performed openly and with total transparency. You can totally check the math to see if the numbers are correct and make sense to you. As you do it, the logic of the AFFF will become even clearer to you. I believe this is the best proof I can give you about the method.

And I would also like to let you play with your own numbers in the Excel sheet to simulate your own journey to financial freedom.

Below, just so you can see it in action for other people, I will share and comment on the Flightplans of four very different individuals – Bob, Aline, Mario, and Ting – who came from different walks of life. When they first simulated their own journeys, they were at different starting points in terms of savings, income, wealth, life circumstances, goals and dreams. I will present their Flightplan projected results here, but you will have the Excel sheets to see the math and all the formulas used. You are more than welcome to challenge me if you disagree with anything, or perhaps you may have suggestions for improvement.

In addition, you will also be able to put in your own numbers to simulate your very own Flightplan.

Please register at my author website at:
www.acceleratedfinancialfreedom.com
to download the Excel sheet called "**Flightplan Simulator.**"

The personal financial freedom journeys of Bob, Aline, Mario, and Ting

The projected AFFF journey for people from different walks of life

The AFFF is a method, and as such, different users will experience it in different ways. Some people will start from a more advantageous point than others. These people may already have a sizeable amount of savings and/or a high income. Others may have little or no savings and a lower income. The AFFF method can be used equally by both groups. The experience will be somewhat different as well as the results. **The AFFF's promise is to accelerate the speed of the journey to achieve financial freedom faster with less money required when compared to mainstream traditional methods.** In my view, it's undeniably a huge advantage. But the AFFF doesn't make any magic. It won't magically make someone on minimum wage and zero savings achieve financial freedom in a few weeks. If that is what you are expecting, I'm sorry to disappoint you. Honestly, I don't know anything that could perform such magic. If someone offers you such a thing, you should be suspicious.

Like any trip you make, the time to your destination will depend on the route you choose, travel distance, road conditions, means of transportation, your own ability, and there is always an element of luck (good and bad). The same happens with your journey to financial freedom. The final actual speed of your own journey will depend on the route you choose (which financial freedom method you chose), travel distance (how much money you need to accumulate in assets from your current savings plus how much you can save along the way, to reach your Target Capital, necessary to produce your Target Income), road conditions (what kind of economic conditions and markets you will encounter: growth or recession), means of transportation (single asset or multi-asset), your own ability (your implementation of the method, how you execute each step), and element of luck (yes, in everything we do in life, there is this random variable we don't control, called luck).

I will present the AFFF Flightplans of four very different people: Bob, Aline, Mario, and Ting (not real names to protect their identities). They come from widely different walks of life. They are middle class but at different levels of income and wealth. As you will see, the time they would take to reach their self-designated financial freedom (different people have different goals, which can be changed in the future at any time, of course) will vary considerably. But one thing is 100% certain for all of them: the AFFF does accelerate their projected journeys compared to any other methods they have ever thought of adopting. Each of them shortlisted two types of assets to simulate for Stage II - Income:

- real estate (with leverage) or
- autorun small business (with leverage)

In addition, they also shortlisted three types of assets to simulate for Stage I - Growth:

- 60/40 portfolio
- Outperform Level I
- Outperform Level II

Important note about assumptions made: For their Flightplans, we made the following assumptions: real estate (cap rate 7%, loan rate 3%, 30Y, LTV 80%, business with valuation 3x ODI, loan rate 8%, 5Y, LTV 60%), and for the Stage I (60/40 portfolio 7.86%, Outperform Level I 11.80%, Outperform Level II 30.10%, all historical average annual returns) for flight simulation purposes to elaborate a Flightplan. **It is important to understand that for all financial plans because they make projections for the future, assumptions must be made.** Generally, we assume the numbers seen in the recent past will repeat in the future. We also generally and simplistically assume the same rate of return to repeat year after year. This is common practice among financial practitioners. But obviously, the future reality will likely turn out different from the assumptions made. A person's savings rate may also change over time. However, in our case, it really doesn't matter because we are doing a **comparative analysis between different methods**. We are not projecting some future value alone but comparing projections. The results will be relative, not absolute. **My goal is to demonstrate and prove that the AFFF is capable of delivering the same desired Target Income for financial freedom multiple times over faster than traditional methods.**

For the results, we will compare journey times of each of the above combinations with the traditional financial method (**the 4% Rule or Rule of 25 and invested in a 60/40 portfolio**).

Bob: Rich but low or no income, wants to maintain lifestyle, reach financial freedom, and have income security (this is common for retirees or near retirement, older folks)

<table>
<tr><td rowspan="3">BOB: 51 years-old, male, family of 4, unemployed but used to have a high income and saved a decent amount of money. He is now unsure about his future because he hasn't been able to land a desirable job since he was laid off. He believes his age is playing a role against him in his line of work. Living off this money scares him off because he doesn't believe it will last long enough. He is desperately looking for ways to reach financial freedom.</td><td>Current savings:</td><td>$500,000</td></tr>
<tr><td>Est. savings rate:</td><td>$0 /month</td></tr>
<tr><td>Target Income:</td><td>$300,000 /year</td></tr>
<tr><td>Traditional method (4% Rule): 60/40 Portfolio ➔</td><td colspan="2">36 years (he'd be 87 by then!)</td></tr>
</table>

The AFFF Method Results		
Stage II assets ➔ **🡻 Stage I assets**	**Real estate + leverage**	**Autorun Small Biz + leverage**
60/40 Portfolio	19 years (1.9x faster)	4 years (9x faster)
Outperform Level I	13 years (2.8x faster)	3 years (12x faster)
Outperform Level II	6 years (6.0x faster)	2 years (18x faster)

Aline: White-collar professional, mid-high income, wants non-work-related passive income for financial freedom and to even retire early, if she wants

<table>
<tr><td rowspan="3">ALINE: 31 years-old, female, family of 2, high income and some good savings. She loves her job and wants to work because she enjoys it and not because she needs to. She decided to secure her financial freedom while she is still young with good earnings and saving power, without having to be too frugal or living below her means. She wants to enjoy life and not be constrained by future uncertainties.</td><td>Current savings:</td><td>$200,000</td></tr>
<tr><td>Est. savings rate:</td><td>$1,500 /month</td></tr>
<tr><td>Target Income:</td><td>$250,000 /year</td></tr>
<tr><td>Traditional method (4% Rule): 60/40 Portfolio ➔</td><td colspan="2">36 years (she'd be 67 by then…)</td></tr>
</table>

The AFFF Method Results		
Stage II assets ➔ **🡻 Stage I assets**	**Real estate + leverage**	**Autorun Small Biz + leverage**
60/40 Portfolio	20 years (1.8x faster)	8 years (4.5x faster)
Outperform Level I	15 years (2.4x faster)	7 years (5.1x faster)
Outperform Level II	8 years (4.5x faster)	4 years (9.0x faster)

Mario: Blue-collar professional, mid-low income, wants financial security from non-work-related income and financial freedom to survive during rough times

MARIO: 27 years-old, male, single, self-employed working in the construction industry. He can find jobs often, but he has no safety net and not much in savings. He has small credit card balances to deal with. He is worried about his financial security and dreams of financial freedom but has no clue where to start. He said he couldn't afford financial advisors, and because of his inconstant income and lack of savings, bankers only offered him CDs and savings accounts with low returns.	**Current savings:**	$0
	Est. savings rate:	$1,000 /month
	Target Income:	$100,000 /year
Traditional method (4% Rule): 60/40 Portfolio ➔	38 years (he'd be 65 by then)	

The AFFF Method Results		
Stage II assets ➔ **🡻 Stage I assets**	**Real estate + leverage**	**Autorun Small Biz + leverage**
60/40 Portfolio	23 years (1.7x faster)	12 years (3.2x faster)
Outperform Level I	18 years (2.1x faster)	10 years (3.8x faster)
Outperform Level II	11 years (3.5x faster)	7 years (5.4x faster)

Ting: young, recent college grad, wants to start her journey to financial freedom early

TING: 24 years-old, female, single, recent college graduate with student loans. She doesn't have any savings and can't save much every month for at least a few years until she gets pay raises at work. She also considers going back to school at some point for her masters, but she is afraid she might not be able to afford it. Financial freedom would provide her a better sense of financial security. She isn't looking for a high passive income yet. Since she is so young, she has time to build on her previously achieved financial freedom for higher levels of income later.	**Current savings:**	$0
	Est. savings rate:	$500 /month
	Target Income:	$60,000 /year
Traditional method (4% Rule): 60/40 Portfolio ➔	40 years (she'd be 64 by then…)	

The AFFF Method Results		
Stage II assets ➔ **⬇ Stage I assets**	**Real estate + leverage**	**Autorun Small Biz + leverage**
60/40 Portfolio	25 years (1.6x faster)	13 years (3.1x faster)
Outperform Level I	20 years (2.0x faster)	12 years (3.3x faster)
Outperform Level II	12 years (3.3x faster)	8 years (5.0x faster)

All these numbers can be found in the Excel workbook called "Flightplan Simulator" that you can download for free. To do so, please register at my author website to download the Excel sheet called

"Flightplan Simulator": www.acceleratedfinancialfreedom.com. You can verify and audit all the formulas yourself. Any comments, questions, suggestions, and challenges are welcome. There is nothing in life that is perfect, and we do want to keep improving!

Now, how about you? You can also put in your own numbers to simulate your very own Flightplan.

<table>
<tr><td rowspan="3">YOU:</td><td>Current savings:</td><td>$ ________</td></tr>
<tr><td>Est. savings rate:</td><td>$______ /month</td></tr>
<tr><td>Target Income:</td><td>$_______ /year</td></tr>
<tr><td>Traditional method (4% Rule): 60/40 Portfolio ➔</td><td colspan="2">_____ years</td></tr>
<tr><td colspan="3">The AFFF Method Results</td></tr>
<tr><td>Stage II assets ➔
🡫 Stage I assets</td><td>Real estate + leverage</td><td>Autorun Small Biz + leverage</td></tr>
<tr><td>60/40 Portfolio</td><td>__ years (__x faster)</td><td>__ years (__x faster)</td></tr>
<tr><td>Outperform Level I</td><td>__ years (__x faster)</td><td>__ years (__x faster)</td></tr>
<tr><td>Outperform Level II</td><td>__ years (__x faster)</td><td>__ years (__x faster)</td></tr>
</table>

Remember that you can choose your own assets if you don't like those in the table above. Remember that Stage I assets should be best for capital appreciation (growth), and Stage II assets should be best for the production of income and be easily leverageable. Also always check the markets before making your selection. Good luck!

Important Takeaways

- The AFFF can work for practically everyone from very different life circumstances and goals. As proven mathematically before, the AFFF will always beat traditional methods.
- Wealthier people with high incomes will naturally have an easier and faster journey. However, even if your savings are small and your income or savings rate is also small, don't lose hope. You are not competing with anyone. You are competing with yourself. It's a personal race for a better version of yourself to win.
- The experience for every person is going to be unique because no two persons will have the exact same goals or life circumstances, choose the same assets, and implement their journeys the same way or at the same time.
- The actual number of years to achieve financial freedom may turn out to be different from the projected number of years because actual returns will likely turn out different from projections. This is normal for all financial plans. Remember, this is just a plan.
- If you encounter headwinds in your journey (e.g., a recession, bear markets, etc.), your journey will likely be delayed. But if you encounter tailwinds (e.g., growing economy, bull markets, etc.), your journey will likely be accelerated even faster. It's a

matter of luck, an external factor out of our control, but it will affect your actual speed. No financial plan will be able to simulate these things.

- You may very probably get pay raises and increase your savings rate during your journey. This will certainly increase your speed to financial freedom. Inflation may also distort numbers and require course adjustments in your journey and changes in your Target Capital and Target Income.
- You should use the Flightplan simulation results as a guideline, not as a certainty set in stone.
- Financial freedom is a marathon, not a sprint. It is a life project, one that is worth pursuing.

CHAPTER 7

7. The AFFF will take you way beyond Financial Freedom

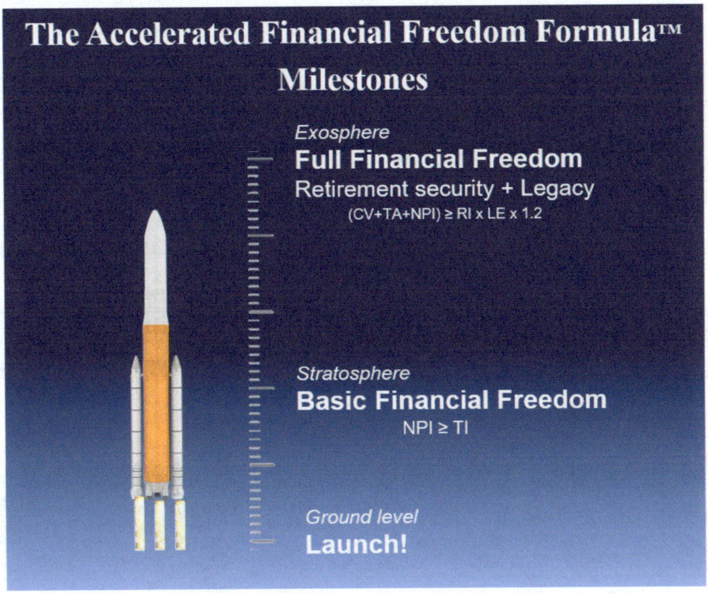

Why? The AFFF is designed not only to guide you to achieve your financial freedom, but to take you **way beyond it**. What is the definition of financial freedom commonly accepted by most authors and the community of financial freedom seekers? Financial freedom, according to this definition, is a condition in a person's life in which all his/her living expenses are paid by a residual income stream that's passive in nature (remember: they work only one time initially to build assets that will pay them income continually into the future). This is generally their definition of financial freedom.

However, my own definition of financial freedom is **much more far-reaching and ambitious**. It comprises two levels of achievement. To make this reading educational, easy to understand, and fun at the same time, I'm using the rocket launch analogy throughout the book. Your journey to financial freedom will be similar to a rocket launch and journey through space.

1st Milestone: BASIC FINANCIAL FREEDOM

Here is the destination where most authors and financial freedom gurus are aiming to take you. It is indeed the most important point in the lives of financial freedom seekers. By having assets generate the same income they get from work, or even more, is huge! It is freedom to choose… where to spend your time, how, with whom, doing what you want, and to do it because you want, not because you need.

The 1st milestone's requirement is that your **Newly-Produced Income by your AFFF assets must be at least equal to or greater than Target Income**:

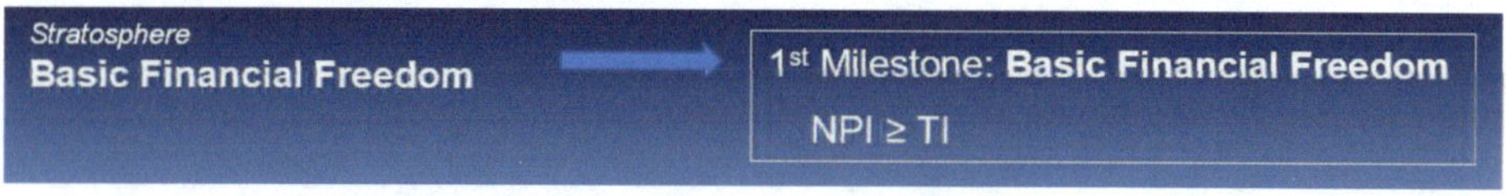

NPI: Newly-Produced Income
TI: Target Income

You may stop here if you want, but I highly recommend you continue on your successful path and keep going a little farther. Why? For two main reasons:

a) As you already know, the income or cashflow from investments may fluctuate. For example, if you are receiving rents, there will be times when your property or properties will be vacant. Sometimes, your tenants will be late paying rents and sometimes you may need to evict them for non-payment. Sometimes, the income from your business may suffer setbacks. Sometimes, the stock market may endure long periods of decline. In other words, no matter what assets you are employing to produce your income, it may suffer temporary fluctuations and even become zero if you rely on a single asset. This is a risk for you. To mitigate this risk, you should do at least one of three things:

1) First, **aim higher than Target Income**, e.g., twice Target Income. Keep working on building more assets under the AFFF framework that already proved successful in taking you to your 1st milestone. By getting a higher income than Target Income, you create a cushion of extra income to better weather the downtimes that will invariably happen to all of us at some point over time.
2) Second, **try to diversify asset types** (e.g., having real estate and a small business) or at least, diversify assets within your preferred asset type (e.g., adding more properties in several locations instead of a single one). By diversifying sources of income, you would also mitigate the risk because it's less probable they would all go bad at the same time, if and when it happens.
3) Another way to prevent getting in trouble when income fluctuates is by establishing liquid reserves such as an **emergency fund**. You just set aside cash reserves you can tap into in case you face headwinds with your investments. You can invest your reserves in a savings account, if you wish, but I think the best way is to save and **invest cash reserves inside the cash value of a**

whole life insurance policy. To learn more about how it works, refer to Chapter 9 about the Module 1 - *Accelerate with* OPM/I Money Boosters. Neither a savings account nor the cash value in a whole life insurance will be exposed to the same risks as your other assets; therefore, they work very well as reserves. And this money is still working for you, earning interest, even though it's earmarked as reserves. Do you want more advantages? How about a much higher rate of return than savings accounts? How about the possibility to enable the use of OPM/I to finance your other investments? How about tax advantages (potentially tax free)? How about leaving unused amounts of cash value become death benefit to pass on to your heirs income tax free? How about knowing that this cash reserve inside the life insurance policy is shielded from potential creditors? Is or isn't whole life insurance a better place to store your cash reserves than a bank account?

b) You need to make sure your retirement is secure for the rest of your life. In other words, you must solve the Longevity Risk Problem. People are living longer and longer. You should not count solely on your assets to make sure you will never run out of money while still alive. I am going to discuss the best solutions to solving these problems in just a minute. Keep reading.

The AFFF is designed to take you further into the journey, beyond **Basic Financial Freedom**. It will help you get financial security, while young, and retirement security later on, making sure to mitigate the longevity risk and leave a legacy to your children. For these, you will need to reach the next and final milestone: **Full Financial Freedom**.

2nd (Final) Milestone: FULL FINANCIAL FREEDOM (Retirement Security & Legacy)

Now that you have already become financially independent and built a cushion around it while more financially secure in life, you are ready for the final destination, which I call **Full Financial Freedom**. Remember, being free is priceless, but being safe and secure at the same time is the nirvana. Safety is the real freedom if you think about it. And if we could also help the next generation by giving them a head start in life, that would be the cherry on top.

The greatest challenge at this point is to make sure you will not outlive your income and assets. It's the so-called Longevity Risk Problem. If there is anything no one has a crystal ball for (besides markets), it is the date of death. People are also living longer and longer, with the advancement of science and health care. Nowadays, the greatest fear the majority of retirees and near-retirees have is whether they will outlive their assets. I think people who typically invest in real estate for retirement income fare better than those who rely solely on financial markets for retirement. That is because retirees who live off rents don't need to liquidate their cash cow (meaning, they don't have to sell property for income), but those who withdraw money from stocks and bonds do (remember the Cow and Milk Analogy in Chapter 2). The latter folks are constantly eating into the nest egg itself. The financial industry's assumption is that the rate of withdrawal will not be greater than the growth rate of the portfolio to replace withdrawn money with new money. Therefore, they usually assume the "safe" rate of withdrawal should be 4%. Nowadays, many argue that 4% is not enough for most people and it should be increased to 5% or even 6%. But here is the trouble. The portfolio must earn at least as much for it not to be eaten away gradually or liquidated. This is a real risk, especially if markets don't behave "as expected" and if retirees live too long. The retiree may outlive the portfolio and that would be a real problem.

That is the reason I really dislike these traditional retirement methods. I honestly think this kind of financial planning, retirement planning based on such assumptions, will fail a lot of people. I believe real estate and small businesses to be much better assets to deal with longevity risk.

Visually, this is the retirement planning challenge. The first problem (#1) illustrated in the diagram below is the longevity risk. What happens if you deplete your retirement accounts or assets, and you are still alive? Where will your income come from after retirement? The second problem (#2) with traditional approaches is what do you leave for your heirs? Nothing?

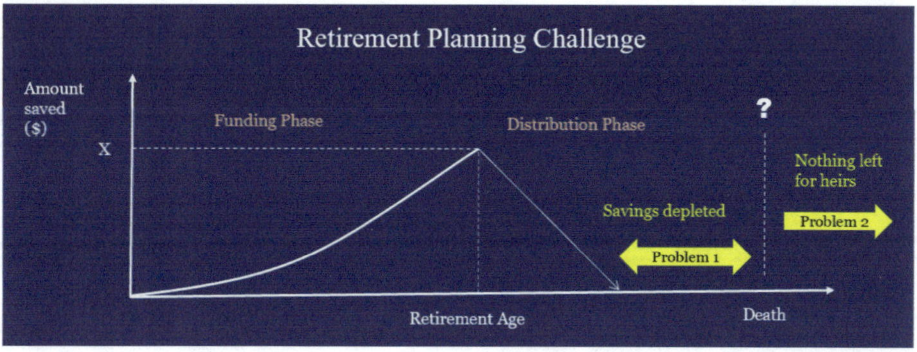

As you can see, for the 4% Withdrawal Rule to work, several things must go right: the stock market must grow way above 4% on average year after year, 4% must be enough to pay for your living expenses (inflation must not go up too much), and you should not live too long, at least not longer than your assets. Wealthy people won't have a problem, but for the rest of the population, if the nest egg is not large enough, this could be a real problem.

The AFFF is based on a different set of principles. We prefer to "drink the milk rather than eating the cow" (The Cow and Milk Analogy, first introduced in Chapter 2). If you are invested in real estate or in autorun small businesses in the Stage II of the AFFF, you will be "drinking milk, not eating the cow." However, to have a complete solution to both problems (#1 and #2), the AFFF has an unbeatable solution, killing both birds with a single stone. There is a very special asset or instrument we have discussed before for OPM/I and in the Module 1 - *Accelerate with* OPM/I Money Boosters (information how to get it in Chapter 9). See the how this special asset solves the problems in the diagram below:

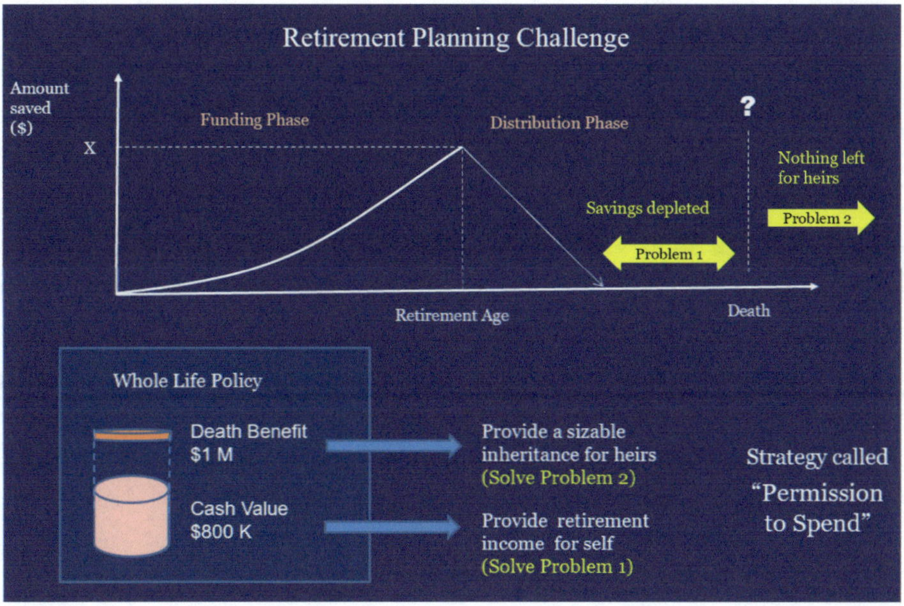

Incorporate the Swiss-Knife of Finance: Whole Life Insurance

A super-important instrument that is often forgotten by some financial planners, perhaps for not being so familiar with how to design it properly, is **whole life insurance**. Many of them offer term life or universal life, which are much weaker choices, in my opinion. The death benefit that these policies offer will help with leaving a legacy for descendants, no doubt. But this solves only problem #2). Unlike whole life, they don't help with the Longevity Risk Problem (problem #1) while you are still alive and possibly running out of money. Whole life solves both problems #1 and #2. It's a strategy called "**Permission to Spend**", which I'm going to explain in a moment.

Term life doesn't even have cash value. Policies are cheap but they have an expiration date. So much for not knowing a person's date of death. How could someone determine what expiration date to choose? Term life does have its uses, but it doesn't help our purposes here, so I would discard it from consideration. Universal life does not offer predictable or guaranteed cash value and death benefit amounts. Premiums are also subject to change. Indexed Universal Life is dependent on the stock market's performance, and its computation is based on so many assumptions that nobody understands, possibly not even their own designers. As I said, universal life does have cash value, but how it changes over time is anyone's guess. I really don't think it's a reliable instrument for our purposes here. I would also discard universal life from consideration.

Whole life is different. First, you will have a predictable, guaranteed death benefit and cash value. If your insurance company pays dividends to you, that is an important extra earning power. Most people choose to reinvest dividends in the policy (instead of cashing them out) so their cash value and death benefit will grow and faster over time. The cash value that accumulates inside the policy will be able to do the following things for you, should you ever need:

- It can be used as collateral for OPM/I so you can borrow the insurance company's money to buy assets to make higher ROI investments;
- It can be used as cash reserves in case of emergencies or loss of income from investments;
- It can be used as an alternative source of retirement income, if necessary.

Let's focus on the 3rd bullet point above for this discussion. Remember Stacey's example in Chapter 5 under the 3rd principle of the AFFF? People who have a fully funded whole life insurance going into retirement will have an **alternative source of income**, should they ever need. By "fully funded," I mean no more premiums due. You would already have a paid-up policy (or policies) by the time you retire, ideally.

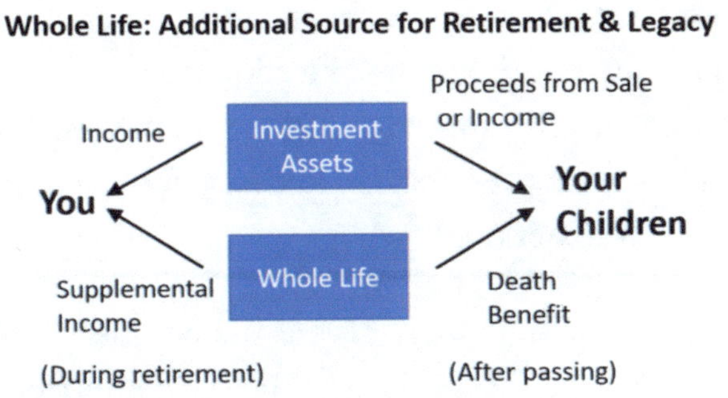

"Permission to Spend" - If you outlive your assets and cash, you may start taking income from your whole life policy as an alternative source. Remember we just discussed storing cash reserves for emergencies inside a whole life policy with numerous advantages over a bank account? It's the exact same principle. It works best if you already have a fully-funded policy (it's important to start the policy early, if possible, while you're young, but it's never too late). You can take money out as withdrawals or as loans that you may never repay the insurance company. Your death benefit will be reduced as a result, but this is a mechanism you can manage (remember Stacey's example in Chapter 5). If you want to take more money out, you will end up leaving less money to descendants as legacy, and vice-versa. You will have control of this balance in your own hands. But the upside is that you will have an additional source of income (supplemental income in retirement) should you need it in life and a sizeable death benefit to pass on to your living descendants.

The "Permission to Spend" Concept

"Permission to Spend" is a concept made possible by the introduction of whole life insurance in a financial retirement plan. As the name suggests, you should be able to spend down your assets during retirement without fear of running out of money in retirement. The central idea behind it is that by the time you have exhausted your assets, the cash value in your policy will cover your income needs for the remainder of your life. I have seen this strategy work even for 70-year-olds already in retirement! The addition of a whole life insurance policy will add an extra source of retirement income that is under your control and has great tax benefits. Let's examine a numerical example so you can see it in action:

The example is hypothetical, but the numbers are real. Let's call him Josh, a 45-year-old male who has accumulated $2,000,000 in assets, and invested in a portfolio that is assumed to earn 4% per year, every year. Let's also assume that Josh also withdraws 4% per year so that the total value of his assets remains fixed at $2,000,000 for simplicity. See the table below:

Year	Age	Assets Beg. Bal.	Growth Rate	Assets Earnings	Withdrawal Rate	Gross Withdrawal	Tax Payment	Net "Income"
1	46	2,000,000	4.0%	80,000	4.0%	80,000	16,000	**64,000**
2	47	2,000,000	4.0%	80,000	4.0%	80,000	16,000	**64,000**
3	48	2,000,000	4.0%	80,000	4.0%	80,000	16,000	**64,000**
4	49	2,000,000	4.0%	80,000	4.0%	80,000	16,000	**64,000**
5	50	2,000,000	4.0%	80,000	4.0%	80,000	16,000	**64,000**
6	51	2,000,000	4.0%	80,000	4.0%	80,000	16,000	**64,000**
7	52	2,000,000	4.0%	80,000	4.0%	80,000	16,000	**64,000**
8	53	2,000,000	4.0%	80,000	4.0%	80,000	16,000	**64,000**
9	54	2,000,000	4.0%	80,000	4.0%	80,000	16,000	**64,000**
51	96	2,000,000	4.0%	80,000	4.0%	80,000	16,000	**64,000**
52	97	2,000,000	4.0%	80,000	4.0%	80,000	16,000	**64,000**
53	98	2,000,000	4.0%	80,000	4.0%	80,000	16,000	**64,000**
54	99	2,000,000	4.0%	80,000	4.0%	80,000	16,000	**64,000**
55	100	2,000,000	4.0%	80,000	4.0%	80,000	16,000	**64,000**
					TOTAL	**4,400,000**	**880,000**	**3,520,000**

If Josh lived to be 100 years old, his investment portfolio would have paid him a total gross amount of $4.4 million, and he would have paid $880,000 in taxes (assuming a tax rate of 20%). This would have netted, after taxes, a total of $3.52 million over 55 years. Upon death, Josh's descendants would inherit the $2 million portfolio. Note that he received $64,000 per year as income well through his retirement years. In summary:

Total gross withdrawal: $4,400,000
Total taxes paid: $880,000
Total net income: $3,520,000

Let's now see how adding a whole life insurance policy would improve his plan in a multitude of ways, allowing Josh to literally spend down his assets and still be better off. Let's examine the table below.

								Whole Life Insurance				
Year	Age	Assets Beg. Bal.	Growth Rate	Assets Earnings	Gross Withdrawal	Tax Payment	Net "Income"	Premiums	Cash Value	D. Benefit	Withdrawal	Loan
1	46	2,000,000	4.0%	80,000	200,000	16,000	84,000	100,000	37,059	1,409,414	0	0
2	47	1,880,000	4.0%	75,200	199,040	15,040	84,000	100,000	102,521	1,425,654	0	0
3	48	1,756,160	4.0%	70,246	198,049	14,049	84,000	100,000	200,462	1,449,456	0	0
4	49	1,628,357	4.0%	65,134	197,027	13,027	84,000	100,000	304,789	1,480,967	0	0
5	50	1,496,465	4.0%	59,859	195,972	11,972	84,000	100,000	415,925	1,520,419	0	0
6	51	1,360,351	4.0%	54,414	194,883	10,883	84,000	100,000	532,296	1,564,540	0	0
7	52	1,219,883	4.0%	48,795	193,759	9,759	84,000	100,000	654,174	1,613,471	0	0
8	53	1,074,919	4.0%	42,997	192,599	8,599	84,000	100,000	781,880	1,667,428	0	0
9	54	925,316	4.0%	37,013	191,403	7,403	84,000	100,000	915,704	1,726,496	0	0
10	55	770,926	4.0%	30,837	190,167	6,167	84,000	100,000	1,056,047	1,790,941	0	0
11	56	611,596	4.0%	24,464	88,893	4,893	84,000	C 0	1,114,151	1,857,568	0	0
12	57	547,167	4.0%	21,887	88,377	4,377	84,000	0	1,175,304	1,926,633	0	0
13	58	480,676	4.0%	19,227	87,845	3,845	84,000	0	1,239,643	1,998,231	0	0
14	59	412,058	4.0%	16,482	87,296	3,296	84,000	0	1,307,356	2,072,536	0	0
15	60	341,244	4.0%	13,650	86,730	2,730	84,000	0	1,378,584	2,149,671	0	0
16	61	268,164	4.0%	10,727	86,145	2,145	84,000	0	1,453,490	2,229,758	0	0
17	62	192,745	4.0%	7,710	85,542	1,542	84,000	0	1,532,195	2,312,921	D 0	0
18	63	114,913	4.0%	4,597	84,919	919	84,000	0	1,615,010	2,399,433	0	0
19	64	34,590	4.0%	1,384	35,974	277	84,000	0	1,651,310	2,415,185	48,303	0
20	65	A 0	0	0	0	0	84,000	0	1,651,879	2,379,030	84,000	0
21	66	0	0	0	0	0	84,000	0	1,652,472	2,343,932	84,000	0
22	67	0	0	0	0	0	84,000	0	1,652,887	2,309,663	84,000	0
23	68	0	0	0	0	0	84,000	B 0	1,653,173	2,276,158	84,000	0
24	69	0	0	0	0	0	84,000	0	1,653,299	2,243,373	84,000	0
25	70	0	0	0	0	0	84,000	0	1,653,254	2,211,296	84,000	0
26	71	0	0	0	0	0	84,000	0	1,652,966	2,179,918	84,000	0
27	72	0	0	0	0	0	84,000	0	1,652,471	2,149,332	84,000	0
28	73	0	0	0	0	0	84,000	0	1,651,711	2,119,507	84,000	0
29	74	0	0	0	0	0	84,000	0	1,650,596	2,090,421	84,000	0
30	75	0	0	0	0	0	84,000	0	1,649,090	2,062,032	84,000	0
31	76	0	0	0	0	0	84,000	0	1,647,168	2,048,139	27,698	56,302
32	77	0	0	0	0	0	84,000	0	1,644,742	2,040,034	0	84,000
33	78	0	0	0	0	0	84,000	0	1,641,759	2,030,646	0	84,000
54	99	0	0	0	0	0	84,000	0	1,069,561	1,151,527	0	84,000
55	100	0	0	0	0	0	84,000	0	1,039,758	1,039,758	0	84,000
				TOTAL	2,684,621	136,924	4,620,000				1,000,001	2,072,302

First, notice how Josh's investment portfolio would be spent down over 19 years (marked in the table as A). Notice also that he'd be able to withdraw a higher amount yearly as income ($84,000 vs. $64,000). This can be seen in the Net Income column in the table marked as B. In addition, notice how the total taxes he'd pay dropped significantly ($136,924 vs. $4,400,000, or if even you want to compare it in the same 19 years period, $304,000, which is still a considerable tax savings). This happens because taxes applied to a shrinking portfolio will naturally diminish with it.

The premiums for Josh's whole life insurance would be fully funded from withdrawals from the portfolio. In other words, Josh wouldn't need any extra dollars to buy and fund the whole life policy.

He'd simply take $100,000 per year from the portfolio to fund his life policy for 10 years, totaling $1 million (marked in the table as C). The whole life policy would instantly provide him a small initial cash value with a $1.4 million death benefit should he pass away that year. Then, year after year, both cash value and death benefit would grow. In the first 19 years of his plan, while Josh would be essentially taking money out of his investment portfolio as income, the whole life policy would be left alone, untouched, just getting funded with $100,000 every year and growing with compound interest.

In year 19, when Josh reaches 64, the investment portfolio would be totally exhausted, and he would no longer get any more money out of it. But this is not a problem because he can switch the source of retirement income from the portfolio to the cash value of his fully funded whole life policy (note: "fully funded" means no more premiums due).

At that moment, in year 19, Josh would have $1.6 million in cash value. Josh would have a choice to take withdrawals from the cash value (also called "surrender") or loans from the insurance company (OPM/I). He could also do both. I personally prefer loans over surrenders, but let's illustrate how he would do both so you can understand how it works. See the area marked as D in the table above.

In this case, Josh would withdraw up to "basis," which is the total amount of premiums he injected into the policy ($1 million). For the IRS, this money would not be taxable because they regard it as a "return of premium." Any further withdrawals will cause taxation to be triggered. So, Josh will switch to loans. In his example, this switch would occur in year 31. For being loans, it is technically not income because loans are supposed to be paid back. Therefore, it wouldn't be taxed either. But, as we already know, you are not required to pay back policy loans. If you pass away without paying back policy loans, the insurance company will simply deduct your balance due from the death benefit to be paid to your designated beneficiaries. Let's now summarize everything and compare with the case without whole life insurance so you can see the differences:

	Without Whole Life	With Whole Life
Total net income taken	3,520,000	4,620,000
Total taxes paid	880,000	136,924
Legacy left to beneficiaries	2,000,000	1,039,758

Note that we are assuming Josh will live to his 100th birthday. The death benefit is projected to change depending on the year of death. Total income and taxes paid would vary too, and you can have an idea by looking at the illustrated numbers year by year.

This is the power of the "Permission to Spend" strategy with whole life insurance. Note: tax laws are subject to change, and you should always consult a licensed tax professional when you design your financial plans.

From the AFFF perspective, the addition of whole life insurance will help tremendously because it can be used as another potential source of income, if necessary, and used as OPM/I to leverage other investments. But most importantly, it can add stability and reliability to your plan.

Leave a Meaningful Legacy to Your Children - Once you have assured your retirement security, solving the Longevity Risk Problem, you may leave an important financial legacy to your children or other successors and beneficiaries. You may leave them your AFFF assets to continue producing income for them or, if they prefer a lump sum of cash instead, sell all the assets. If you have whole life insurance policies, they can also provide a significant amount of cash via death benefit, which will pass income tax free, to your designated beneficiaries. Besides a financial legacy, perhaps the most important and valuable legacy you could leave your children is financial education. Teach them what you have learned throughout your entire journey. Education will probably be the best legacy you can leave them, besides money and assets.

Finally, how do you know you achieved the final milestone, which actually is the final destination of the AFFF journey? The requirement for this final milestone is that **all your income sources and wealth (Cash Value in your whole life policies + Total Assets + Newly-Produced Income by your AFFF assets) must be at least equal to or greater than 1.2x your desired Retirement Income through your Life Expectation**:

CV: Cash Value (whole life insurance)
TA: Total Assets
NPI: Newly-Produced Income
RI: Retirement Income
LE: Life Expectancy

The idea for this final milestone is simple. You want to make sure, to the largest extent possible, that your income and wealth will last as long as you live. Life expectancy is impossible to predict because it's just an average number, and each one of us will live more or less years than that number. Therefore, it's always recommended to add a safety margin. I think 20% is a good safety margin, but you can disagree and use a different number that you are most comfortable with. I agree that this is still an assumption but, in this case, the success of the plan is dependent on a lot less variables than the 4% Rule. Besides, here you would have two sources for money – the assets and the whole life policy – instead of just a single source – the assets – of your 4% Rule account.

CHAPTER 8

8. The Accelerated Financial Freedom Formula TM – A Step by Step Formula

Create your Flightplan with an investment blueprint to reach Financial Freedom

Imagine you are the Chief Flight Director for a rocket launch at NASA like Gene Kranz. You will set the vision and goals for the mission. You will have the finest engineers, astronauts, and personnel at your command. You will have the most modern technology ever developed in the history of mankind built into your rockets, engines, fuel, computers, imaging, telemetry, communications, etc., including up-to-date weather reports, available to you. Before launch day, you will have your team prepare a complete and detailed flight plan. In it, you will also have contingency plans for unexpected things that may potentially compromise the mission.

The same must be done with your journey to financial freedom. The AFFF is designed to take advantage of all available investment types and will help you create an investment blueprint tailored to you, based on your own goals, circumstances, and the prevailing economic context. This investment blueprint will be laid out in your **Flightplan**.

Invariably, as in any trip or mission in life, you will probably face headwinds, challenges, and unexpected (not planned for) things that will require you to make changes in your plan or trajectory during the journey, just like launching a rocket into space. The AFFF is designed to help guide you step by step in an easy way to follow and allows you to reach your financial freedom destination 2x-10x faster than traditional methods with less money required.

The Step-by-Step Formula has 9 steps and is divided in 3 segments – **Pre-Launch, In-Flight,** and **Destination Landing** – just as in a rocket launch! Here is how it is organized with every step in a logical order.

The Accelerated Financial Freedom Formula™
A Step-by-Step Checklist

Pre-Launch

STEP 1	**Self-Assessment**	Know yourself and set your unique vision
STEP 2	**Define Mission Goals**	Define your Target Income
STEP 3	**Check Weather Conditions**	Check trends of economy and markets
STEP 4	**Run Flight Simulation**	Find out your numbers and expectations
STEP 5	**Pilot Training**	Get your financial and investor's education

In-Flight

STEP 6	**Lift Off!**	Launch your Flightplan into action
STEP 7	**Course check/corrections**	Review your investments, markets, milestones
STEP 8	**Structure check**	Asset protection, risk management, tax optimization

Destination Landing – Your Full Financial Freedom (Congrats!)

STEP 9	**Landing**	**Full Financial Freedom** with retirement security + leave a legacy

---

Let's now describe each of the steps.

* * * PRE-LAUNCH * * *

Pre-Launch is the phase when you plan your journey. You must first understand yourself, set the vision for your future, and get yourself mentally ready to execute your plans.

STEP 1: Self-Assessment

The very first step of any planning process starts with yourself. First of all, you must know yourself. Here is a brief self-knowledge exercise you can do to get started.

You will find the **Self-Assessment Questionnaire** in the Appendix or download it from my author website as a printable PDF. It has 20 questions to map out where you are, where you want to go, who you are, what you are comfortable with, what you are proficient at doing, etc. Take some time alone with your thoughts somewhere quiet without distractions to reflect on these important self-assessment questions and write down your answers. They will give you a more concrete sense of purpose you can use to prepare for the next step of your **Flightplan**.

Note that there are no right or wrong answers. The Self-Assessment Questionnaire will help you see more clearly the potential paths ahead of you. Keep your answers handy. You will need them in STEP 4, when you start choosing the asset types for the Stages I and II of your AFFF Flightplan.

STEP 2: Define the Goals of your Mission

After reflecting upon your needs, dreams, and goals for the future during the Self-Assessment step, you should have a pretty good idea what the goals should be of your mission with the AFFF. Note that you don't need a definitive Target Income because it can be revised in the future should your circumstances and goals change. Life changes and so should plans adjust accordingly. In addition, even if you defined a Target Income a little too aggressively or too conservatively, you could always make course corrections along the way. Therefore, what is important is to have a defined goal right now to focus on: your own **Target Income**.

Your Target Income should not only be able to cover all your monthly expenses today, but also try to include any anticipated expenses in your foreseeable future. If you don't have any projections for future expenses, you may add 10-20% to your current expenses, assuming that would be more or less the right number. Also, note that for simplicity, we are not considering income taxes here because everyone's situation will be unique and tax rates may change anyway. Finally, remember that investment income may fluctuate. For example, if you are making rental income, there may be months that you will have a vacancy or some late payments, so these things will make your income fluctuate. For all these reasons, it's always a good idea to add an extra safety margin. Again, be flexible and make adjustments as this becomes clearer to you. Once you determine your number, write it down below:

My Target Income is: $__________ per month

(or $_____________ per year).

It's important to write down our goals and plans. It helps us stay focused and it becomes a constant reminder in a world of so many distractions.

Remember, this is the Target Income that will take you to reach your **Basic Financial Freedom**. It's an important milestone in your journey. It means all your living expenses will be covered by income generated by your investments.

STEP 3: Check Weather Conditions

This is not only a must for all air travel and space mission launches, but it is also a must for any investments! You don't need to do a complete study or a deep analysis of the state of the economy or each market, but you have to know in general what is going on out there. A simple overview is sufficient. For example, you should be able to answer the following questions:

1) **Economy** – What's going on: is the economy growing or stagnating?

2) **Interest rates** – Are they considered high or low right now? Are they going up or down?

3) **Stock prices** - Are we on a bull or bear market right now? What are analysts forecasting?

4) **Real estate prices** - Are they considered high or low right now? Are they going up or down? Can you find regional or local markets at more favorable points in the cycle?

5) **Rents** - Are they considered high or low right now? Are they going up or down?

Basically, you need to have a view for the above indicators as to where they currently sit and where they are heading (trends). That's all. It's not difficult. You can read it in the papers.

Economic Fundamentals

Interest rates 1-month view	Inflation 6-month view	Econ. growth 1-year view
Too high	Too high	On fire
Increasing	Increasing	Accelerating
Neutral	Neutral	Neutral
Decreasing	Decreasing	Decelerating
Too low	Too low	Recession

Real Estate Investing

Prices 1-year view	Rents 1-year view
Emerging	Too high
Appreciating	Increasing
Turning point	Neutral
Depreciating	Decreasing
Recession	Too low

Stock Market Investing

Current For the day	Trend 1-month view	Trend 1-year view
Very Bullish	Very Bullish	Very Bullish
Bullish	Bullish	Bullish
Neutral	Neutral	Neutral
Bearish	Bearish	Bearish
Very Bearish	Very Bearish	Very Bearish

Fixed Rate Bond Investing

Current For the day	Trend 1-month view	Trend 1-year view
Very Bullish	Very Bullish	Very Bullish
Bullish	Bullish	Bullish
Neutral	Neutral	Neutral
Bearish	Bearish	Bearish
Very Bearish	Very Bearish	Very Bearish

(Views as of January 10, 2023)

If you are too busy to study the economy and markets in-depth or you are just not very proficient in this, it is okay. You don't need to dig much deeper than just having a general feeling where markets are and where they are likely heading. It is similar to reading the weather forecast when planning for a trip. You don't need to be a meteorologist. You just need to know what meteorologists are forecasting for the weather, so you can make more informed decisions, rather than going out blindly.

STEP 4: Run the Flight Simulation: simulate your own path to financial freedom

Now it's time for you to simulate your own path to financial freedom! First, you need to download the **Flightplan Simulator.xlsx Excel sheet** from my author website if you haven't already: www.acceleratedfinancialfreedom.com.

Next, you will need to pick at least an asset for each of the two stages of AFFF: Stage I and Stage II. Remember, Stage I is to help you reach Target Capital faster and Stage II is the OPM-powered income generator that will ultimately produce for you the Target Income you want. Review the AFFF framework below:

THE ACCELERATED FINANCIAL FREEDOM FORMULA™ FRAMEWORK

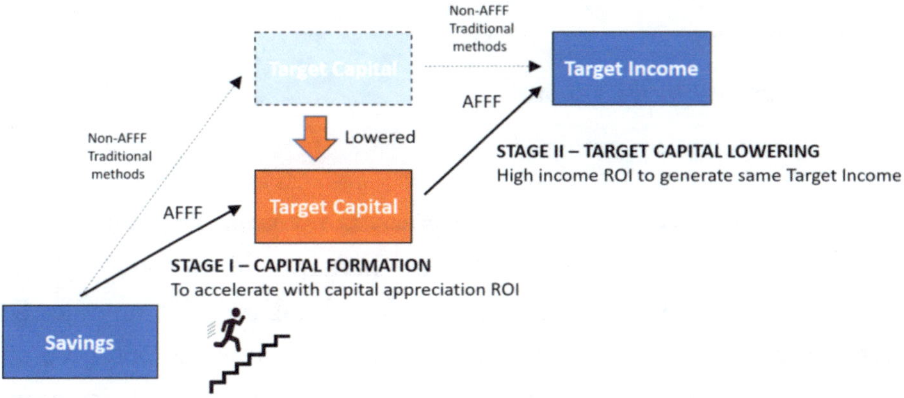

The Accelerated Financial Freedom Formula ™ Multi-Asset Approach: Asset type choices (suggested)

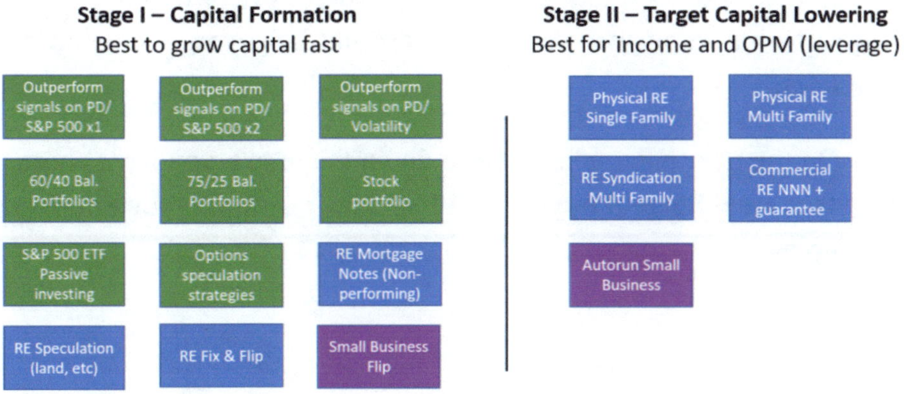

Now is the time you need to select your assets. To help select the best assets for your situation, I showed you how to do it in Chapter 5. Please review first the menu of commonly used assets in Chapter 5. To make a decision, you will need to think about each of these aspects and how they fit your needs and circumstances (review your Self-Assessment Questionnaire, if necessary):

- Amount of money required
- Yield
- Passiveness
- Easiness
- Stability of the income
- Appreciation potential

If you have difficulty choosing assets for your Flightplan, seek help. By the way, if you experience difficulty in any step of this process, you should immediately seek help. Don't let any hurdle become a roadblock for your financial freedom journey and give up on your dreams! You can attend my online workshops to learn more about the practical aspects of the AFFF's implementation. Check **STEP 5 – Pilot Training** for details on my further training with workshops and mentorship programs where you will have direct access to me to answer your questions and help you overcome the obstacles.

On the next page, please write down the assets you have chosen for Stage I and Stage II of your AFFF and the results of your simulated Flightplan:

MY SIMULATED FLIGHTPLAN

My Stage I – Capital Formation Asset(s) will be:

______________________________________.

My Stage II – Target Capital Lowering Income-Producing Asset(s) will be: ____-
____.

Briefly explain why you made these choices (important for you to remember in the future because your plans must be flexible and may be changed as needed): _______________________________________
____
____
____.

RESULTS:

Target Income: $____________ /year

Target Capital reduced from $___________________________ to
$________________________ (___% reduction)

Journey time for 4% Rule method: _____ **years** (Target Capital
$________________________)

Journey time for AFFF with ___________________________:
_____ **years (____x faster)**

(My chosen assets)

How about OPM/I? When should I start investing in Whole Life Insurance?

We used OPM/E for Stage II assets. But what about OPM/I? As commented earlier, unless you already have a whole life insurance policy fully funded with cash value (I'm assuming you don't), OPM/I will not help you accelerate your financial freedom at the beginning of your journey, but it will add stability to it (by offering an extra income source) and really accelerate the final stages of your journey. So, if you are very young and you are eager to arrive as soon as possible, you may choose not to invest in a whole life policy right at the very beginning of your journey, but you should consider starting to fund a new policy as soon as possible.

The good news is that you can even start with a tiny policy at any time to learn how it works and feel its power. You may always add new policies as you grow your assets and increase your newly-produced income. By the way, you can use this new income to fund the premiums of your whole life policy. You can find more details about how this works in the Money Boosters and OPM/I Module (information how to get the contents, in written format and in video, in Chapter 9 or Chapter 11) but you need to know that part of your premiums will become cash value and that it's going to get invested and grow over time. With cash value as collateral, you may access loans from the insurance company to fund your new asset purchases. This is OPM/I.

Since cash value takes time to grow, you will realize the full power of the OPM/I booster later in your journey. But it's never too early or too late to start. It's like planting a tree. It takes time for it to grow. *"The best time to plant a tree was 20 years ago. The next best time is now."* Don't forget to include whole life insurance in your

Flightplan. You choose when you should start adding it but better do it sooner rather than later.

STEP 5: Pilot Training

If many things discussed so far in the book are new to you and if you are feeling a little overwhelmed by the information you have been reading, it is a good sign because it means you are learning something new! But it is also a sign that you probably need some "Pilot Training." I have tried to avoid industry jargon and write in a way most people, non-financial professionals, would understand. However, people come from different walks of life and have had different degrees of exposure to the financial and investment world. Most people simply had no financial education whatsoever when they were in school. I was one of those people. I only learned finance after I started working for a bank as a junior financial analyst.

Unfortunately, most people get their financial and investment education the wrong way. They get it from the sellers of financial or investment products. How biased do you think that kind of information would be? When you see commercials on TV, that is sell-side's information. This is one of the main reasons why you only learn about single-asset investments. No wonder, it's "coincidentally" the one they are selling you! I bet I may be the first suggesting that you broaden your horizons and think multi-asset. Am I? That's why proper financial education is paramount.

All of us have our own strengths and weaknesses. All of us will be very good at some things and do poorly at other things. All of us have blind spots in our knowledge of something, even if we are experts in the subject. It's impossible for us to know everything. But that is perfectly fine. We just need to recognize what we need help with and get that help. For example, you might be a day trader who feels very confident at trading stocks but knows next to nothing about real estate. You should bridge that gap with specific real estate investing education. Some other people may be very far from the finance world and need more comprehensive help in all aspects of finance and investing. That is fine, too. These folks should seek general but also specific education on multiple finance and financial markets topics.

The important point of STEP 5 is to pause and reflect on your own abilities to implement the AFFF. Are you ready to start? Do you see areas you need help with? This is the moment to think about it. You are still in the project's pre-launch phase of the project so this is the time to ensure everything is well-prepared before the launch. If you need to learn more (general or specific) before starting the implementation of your AFFF, that is absolutely fine. You are not alone. We have all been there.

Besides the book, as I said, additional educational opportunities will help with your preparation. I had initially planned to include one chapter, which I called Module, for each major asset type (financial markets, real estate, small business), a special chapter about Money Boosters, and another special chapter about asset protection, risk management, and tax optimization techniques. But halfway through writing the book, I realized I had already written so much content that it would be too much for one book. Therefore, I decided to split away the Modules from this book. I should publish them separately (in a series, perhaps) after publishing this book, which is to be focused exclusively on the AFFF method.

However, you don't have to wait for these books to be published. Just tour my author website, and you will find a menu of content in the form of video courses, workshops, and even mentorship programs, for those who prefer a closer interaction to guide them through their financial freedom journeys. In other words, I offer you all the support should you need it. I can help you implement your AFFF journey in a few different ways, depending on what you need and what works best for you.

In Chapter 9, you will read more details about each of the Modules mentioned earlier as well as instructions on how to access **free video content** (it's a bonus for you for purchasing my book):

- **Module 1:** *Accelerate with* Money Boosters: Optimize Use of Money
- **Module 2:** *Accelerate with* Real Estate Investments
- **Module 3:** *Accelerate with* Stock Market
- **Module 4:** *Accelerate with* Autorun Small Business
- **Special Workshop:** Introduction to the Accelerated Financial Freedom Formula™
- **Special Booklet:** Asset Protection, Risk Management, and Tax Optimization

In Chapter 11, you will find information about training programs through video courses, recorded and live workshops, mentorship, and other resources, to help you throughout your journey to financial freedom.

*** * * IN-FLIGHT * * ***

STEP 6: Lift-Off!

Now that you have completed the 5 Pre-Launch Steps, you are ready to launch!

Good luck and bon voyage!

The first destination is your **Basic Financial Freedom**.

Start building up your assets, one at a time, that you have selected in STEP 4, when you planned and simulated your journey. Normally, you should start from Stage I, but if you already have your Target Capital in hand, great, you can skip Stage I. Some people are wealthier or had already saved earlier and are ready for Stage II.

If you have questions or encounter problems in the implementation of your financial freedom journey under the AFFF framework, you can always go back to STEP 5 and seek more education with specific courses (on each type of asset), attend a workshop or enroll in a mentorship program, if you want to ask me your specific questions, get guidance, receive feedback on your progress, or find coaching to help you implement AFFF to reach your financial freedom.

If you are feeling anxious or even fearful of launching, it's normal. That happens because it is an important journey on which you are about to embark. I'm sure you will encounter challenges along the way because it is normal, too. We all do. I would be lying to you if I said it's going to be just a breeze. In life, nothing comes easy or in a straight line. If someone offers you easy money schemes, it's probably a scam. But we are well equipped with our intellect to face all the challenges that come our way. It's been like this for thousands or even millions of years as humans have become the dominant species on this planet. Remember, you don't need to be perfect to reach your destination. Even the best sports teams win championships with a few losses and let opponents score too. You just need to stay focused on your targets. Check the weather often and make necessary course adjustments. A little luck would be always welcome, like in any endeavor that matters in life. And you should be successful. If you have done your homework well through the initial 5 Pre-Launch Steps, I fully trust you will reach your goals and claim your financial freedom.

Once you reach your first milestone – your **Basic Financial Freedom** - you should be earning your **Target Income**, which should cover all your living expenses. If you have a day job and wish to quit, you could, from the income standpoint, as your investment income should be able to replace the wages from your job.

With **Basic Financial Freedom**, you will already be at a very enviable position to exercise your newly found freedom in your life. And congratulations for all your efforts and determination to reach this point. While most people only dream about financial freedom, you actually achieved it. You got there! You should really be proud of yourself. But you should not stop there!

Once you get there, you want to solidify this position. The best way to do this is to add more margin for safety, meaning additional income. You will also want to add more safety reserves for emergencies and other unexpected needs. By reserves I don't mean leaving a truckload of money in a savings account earning the minimum interest rate. There are better ways to do this, e.g., starting (if you don't have already) a whole life insurance policy. This way, you start building the foundations to use **OPM/I** in the future. The cash value inside the policy grows at a much higher earnings rate than a savings account, and it's very secure if you choose a solid insurance company. For more information about this, please refer to instructions in Chapter 9. If you already own whole life policies, you may add more if you have excess reserves. Remember that although OPM/I won't accelerate your journey initially, it will do so at later stages of your journey and add stability to it. That is another reason a whole life insurance policy will be necessary to solve another big problem in the future: the longevity risk problem and achieving retirement security. This will be the 2nd and last milestone in your journey: **Full Financial Freedom**. Whole life insurance will play an essential role in its implementation.

STEP 7: Course Check / Course Corrections

This step does not need to be long or difficult to execute. In your journey, you should often check the progress of your implementation of the AFFF.

The external environment may have changed since you launched your journey. The economy may have improved or deteriorated. Interest rates may have gone up or down. Inflation may have changed too. The stock market may have entered a different regime, bull or bear. The real estate market where you are currently investing may have changed to a new stage in the local cycle. New, promising real estate markets may have emerged in other locations, creating fresh opportunities. That's exactly why I keep emphasizing we should keep an eye on the changing context. It's just like checking the weather. Even during the journey, we must check external conditions and make necessary adjustments to our Flightplan.

Checking markets regularly does not mean that we must chase every market movement that comes our way. At the same time, we don't have to catch every investment opportunity that comes to us. Therefore, we should not change our entire Flightplan all the time with the changing markets. We should stick to our plans but make adjustments as necessary. Adjustments are usually minor, unless the changes in external factors are so monumental that they require a totally new Flightplan. It's like a course correction pilots make in response to turbulence. They don't toss their original flight plan away but they make course adjustments.

Some adjustments may include asset rebalancing, rotation, or substitution. In light of what is going on in the markets and their trends, you may want to change some assets in your portfolio by selling them for new ones. The reasons are many. For example, taxes may have changed. The government may have increased taxation for some types of investments, while reducing for other types. Another reason might be that you have incurred large taxable gains you want to offset with losses holding other similar assets to pay less taxes overall. Another example is that you invest in sector stocks and the economy changed, making some sectors more promising than others. Or perhaps you are a growth stock investor and interest rates surged, making these stocks particularly risky, and you want to rotate your growth stocks to value stocks. These are just a few examples, but there are many reasons why you may want to make course corrections from time to time.

There is another thing that may motivate an asset substitution. If you are a real estate investor, you must keep an eye not only on your current cashflow but also try to anticipate future maintenance requirements. For example, some investment properties you own may need a costly renovation at some point in the future. You will anticipate this event and sell it before renovation needs become too apparent. You may use the proceeds to buy another similar property in better shape elsewhere. Another example is that a small business owner may anticipate his/her competitive landscape is about to change, perhaps with new competitors moving in or a new technology that might disrupt the demand for their products and decides to sell the business before these things start to cause problems. These are all good reasons to revise your Flightplan and make necessary course corrections.

Learning and education may also trigger a course correction. For example, you started the journey as a newbie real estate investor. You invested in some high ROI properties that were located in a pretty rough area of town. Over time, you realized that you have faced numerous challenges with tenant delinquencies or perhaps with a city that wasn't landlord-friendly. The realized ROI was below expected

ROI, and this is frustrating. You realized you made a few mistakes and learned from them. You decided to sell these properties and buy elsewhere. This is perfectly normal, and learning is part of life. It's okay to make mistakes. I certainly made a lot of them! Only those who make mistakes can learn and get smarter and more successful. But no sweat. Learn, make course corrections, and move on!

Continuing education in new fields of knowledge can launch us into experimentation. For example, real estate investors who were fearful of investing in the stock market may realize, after more education, that it is not as difficult nor the 7-headed monster they once had thought it was and decide to try it out. It's a good idea to start small. Trial and error. And learn from each trial. Most people freak out at the idea of running a small business. They think they will be embroiled in a never-ending streak of headaches resulting in losses and frustrations. Of course, people do have preferences and no asset is equally attractive to everyone, but education can make a huge difference.

I practice intermittent fasting for health reasons. From time to time, I embark on a block water fast, which may take several days. I started with a 3-day water fast, and over the years, I extended the fasting period to as long as 7 days. Many people think I'm crazy. Friends said they would never be able to fast, or they would die. I say you can, and you won't die. You just have not tried. Fasting is hard, but it gave me so many positives I could not get in any other way. The same logic applies here. I encourage people to try new things they have never done before. To feel the fear is normal. With proper education and a little determination, you can do it. Be disciplined and responsible, though. Start small and experiment. Only scale up after you dominated the skill.

All these examples about making course corrections prove why checking the weather often is so important. Investing passively on a static rule of thumb is easy but leads to poor results and can even spell disaster if the worse combination of factors catch you unprepared. We have all witnessed what happened during the 2000 and 2008 financial crises, how much damage these market crashes did to people's lifetime savings. The weather was changing outside, and people were still investing the traditional way, totally unprepared for what was about to come. The irony is that it did not happen overnight and talk of imminent financial disaster was all over the news for weeks. Still, people walked blindfolded into the crises and lost big, especially those with a lifetime of savings stuck in rigid 401k plans. We must always be aware of the environment around us. Static rules of thumb only work in certain, usually too optimistic, scenarios, assuming everything works as expected. But we know life is not like that. External factors are things we don't control. We can't control the wind, but we can adjust the sails to keep us on course to reach our financial freedom.

STEP 8: Structural Check – Asset Protection, Risk Management, and Tax Optimization

A mission to space always requires a structural check once the space module reaches orbit. The crew needs to make sure no damage was done to the structure during launch and that the returning capsule will withstand the infernal heat of reentry. We must do the same with our investments. We must make sure our assets are protected from all forms of 'damage.' Are our assets exposed to known and unknown risks we cannot tolerate? What are the risk factors that may cause our assets to lose value? Can someone steal or damage our properties? Can we be sued and lose our assets as a result? These are all important questions because, while we are busy saving money and building assets, we may be exposed to lose them all. There are many asset protection and risk management techniques I have learned over the years.

Besides asset protection and risk management, one significant wealth eroding factor in our lives is called TAXES. Unfortunately, the government is your partner in everything you do, whether you like it or not. If you made money, Uncle Sam wants a share. Even if you aren't yet sure whether you made money, the government still wants its share upfront in form of quarterly estimated taxes, or it will charge penalties and late fees. But if you lose money, it will not share your losses, only your gains. I am not against government and social benefits to needy people, but taxes are just way too 'taxing' to people. You work so hard to save and build assets, only to see a large portion of it disappear due to taxes. Therefore, we must work smarter. You should never ever evade your tax obligations (it's a crime!) but use the legal loopholes allowed by the tax code itself to pay the minimum tax you are required to pay. This is the playbook of the rich in this country (and the rest of the world too for that matter). They legally optimize their businesses and investments to minimize losses to taxation.

You will often hear the pair of terms **Asset Protection and Tax Optimization** together because you would usually use a solution to solve both problems at the same time. For anyone on the road to financial freedom, these two are absolutely important topics, so I must cover at least the basics. I'm going to briefly discuss some concepts here, but more details will be provided in a special Booklet to be published but also included as a BONUS for you here. Check out Chapter 9 or Chapter 11 on how to get your free copy.

Asset Protection, Risk Management, and Tax Optimization

Let's start with Asset Protection and Risk Management. The problem is that you may lose money and even entire assets. Let's discuss some common problems and how they are usually solved or mitigated. Again, let me make the disclaimer: **I'm not an attorney, nor a CPA or tax specialist**. I'm just sharing what I have learned over the years as a user. We all must learn from them and consult with them for their expertise. But I do have extensive risk management experience working for Wall Street banks. Banks deal with risk all the time. Banks buy and sell risks. We don't need the whole playbook banks use, but a sub-set of techniques they use can be very helpful to us as investors.

These two topics are quite extensive and although very important for any and all investors, they are not in the core of the AFFF method. Therefore, I created a separate Booklet called **Asset Protection, Risk Management, and Tax Optimization** that I'm giving away as a free BONUS. You can download it (free) from my author website: check out Chapter 11 for other special bonuses that come with it.

In risk management, I will cover:

- Market Risk
- Credit Risk (or Counterparty Risk)
- Liquidity Risk
- Interest Rate Risk
- Liability Risk (Lawsuits)
- Income Loss from Death Risk
- Property & Casualty Risk
- Business Structure for Asset Protection

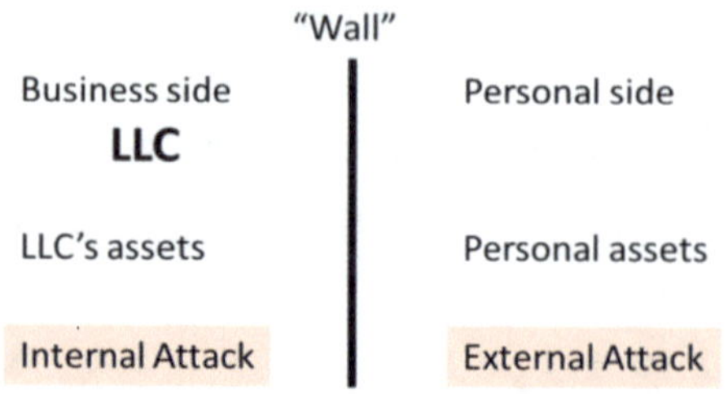

Besides protecting your assets with risk management and insurance, you should also seriously consider incorporating a business structure to shield your assets from potential creditors. For example, a very common structure is the LLC (Limited Liability Company). The "wall" the LLC erects between you and your business shields any attempts by others to get to your assets. I will describe and explain how an LLC protects you, your business, and your assets (investments) in the downloadable booklet.

In addition, I will also discuss some ideas for Tax Optimization. We want to make sure we are paying the least amount of taxes legally, just like the wealthy people do. How we organize and structure our businesses, assets, and investments will make a huge difference in the amount of taxes we will be required to pay.

It's important to understand that taxes are an external factor that we don't control directly. However, just like all other external factors (the economy, markets, etc.), we can control the ways we respond to them. Remember the saying, "*We don't control the wind, but we can adjust the sails.*" This is exactly what we should do with tax optimization. The government sets the rules and we play by the rules, but in a smart way to legally pay the least amount possible.

Taxes are an important wealth-eroding factor. In the long run, what people tolerate as "small contributions" out of their hard-earned income to the government add up imperceptibly to staggering amounts of wealth transfer. Take a look at this table to see the effect. Imagine a dollar ($1.00) doubling every year (100% return per year) for 20 years. It's the same example we used in Chapter 5, but instead of doubling daily, here we assume it doubles annually. We chose an absurdly high return to super-magnify the effect, but you can see it work with any return you want. If such an investment existed, you would have $1,048,576 after 20 years. Now let's tax the earnings every year at a 25% income tax rate.

$1 doubling 20 times

Year	Balance (No Taxes)	Balance (25% Taxes)	Taxes Paid (25% Taxes)
0	1.00	1.00	
1	2.00	1.75	0.25
2	4.00	3.06	0.44
3	8.00	5.36	0.77
4	16.00	9.38	1.34
5	32.00	16.41	2.34
6	64.00	28.72	4.10
7	128.00	50.27	7.18
8	256.00	87.96	12.57
9	512.00	153.94	21.99
10	1,024.00	269.39	38.48
11	2,048.00	471.43	67.35
12	4,096.00	825.01	117.86
13	8,192.00	1,443.76	206.25
14	16,384.00	2,526.58	360.94
15	32,768.00	4,421.51	631.64
16	65,536.00	7,737.64	1,105.38
17	131,072.00	13,540.88	1,934.41
18	262,144.00	23,696.54	3,385.22
19	524,288.00	41,468.94	5,924.13
20	**1,048,576.00**	**72,570.64**	10,367.23
			24,189.88
	976,005.36	total loss	
	24,189.88	tax paid	
	951,815.48	LOC	

You can see that the same investment taxed at 25% resulted in just $72,570.64. The loss is a staggering $976,005.36. Note that this is not only taxes. All the taxes you paid add up to just $24,189.88. But wait! If I paid $24,189.88 in taxes over 20 years, how could it be possible that $976,005.36 disappeared? Well, the largest chunk of losses ($951,815.48) is actually the Lost Opportunity Cost (LOC) that resulted from the taxation. What is this? It is the earnings you would have made if the money you paid in taxes were working for you instead. Remember the magic of compound interest? Well, 25% of it was broken every year! If each dollar paid to the IRS were invested at the same rate of return, instead of paid to the IRS, it would have grown over the years and added up to almost $1 million in this extreme example. In the end, the lost earnings end up many times larger than the amount effectively paid to the IRS. Think about it. You get the idea. Lost Opportunity Cost (LOC) is one of the Money Leaks I discussed in **Module 1-** ***Accelerate with*** **Money Boosters** video (instructions in Chapter 11).

What we lose by paying taxes is not only the taxes themselves, but also the Lost Opportunity Costs (LOC) of not being able to invest those amounts.

Rich people hire tax strategists to figure out legal ways to pay less taxes. You should do the same. Get the financial education you need. It will make a huge difference in your life you probably haven't even realized. There is this famous quote, "*If you think education is expensive, try ignorance*" (Derek Bok). Education is gold; financial education is priceless.

Reminder: Make sure you download my special Booklet (free) with a lot more details on these topics called **Asset Protection, Risk Management, and Tax Optimization.** Find details in Chapter 11.

STEP 9: Landing – Solve the Longevity Problem and Leave a Meaningful Legacy

The last step of your journey to **Full Financial Freedom** consists of making sure two important things are properly handled:

- **Retirement security**: you can only really sleep soundly at night not worried that you might run out of retirement income if you mitigated the Longevity Risk Problem. You want to be financially free, but you also want to make sure it will last for your entire lifetime. No one knows how long they will live. The 4% Rule solves (actually it doesn't) the problem by making projections, assumptions, simulations, etc., about "possible scenarios" for a "safe" withdrawal rate to be 4%, 5% or more, but in the end, they may easily fail. The AFFF solution described in Chapter 4 is much better, solid, and more certain. Certainty is always stronger and preferable to uncertainty.
- **Legacy for the next generation**: you want to leave assets or money for your children, grandchildren, charity, etc., once you pass. In a world in constant change and disruption, you want to give your children the best head start in life you can. You may let them inherit the assets you built under the AFFF framework, so that they may keep receiving income. While this is a good idea, I strongly suggest you consider a whole life insurance, which can give you not only the power of OPM/I to boost investments and extra safety cushion (emergency reserves), but also a sizeable death benefit for your heirs.

Have you taken care of both things already? If yes, you are now ready for landing!

Destination Landing: Your Full Financial Freedom (Congrats!) - If you arrived here, **congratulations** are in order. To arrive here is quite an achievement!

CHAPTER 9

9. (BONUS) The Accelerated Financial Freedom Formula ^{TM} Modules

When I first set out to write this book, my intention was to introduce the AFFF method and dive deep into all the main asset types used by the AFFF. I really wanted you to have a complete view and understanding of the method because I realized that existing methods were so inefficient that most people were simply turned off by them. Then, when I was halfway through writing the book, I took stock of how blessed I was for having had the opportunity to be exposed to and having learned so many different types of investments – ranging from financial markets (stocks, bonds, currencies, interest rates, derivatives, etc.) to real estate (single family, multi-family, mortgage notes, syndication, etc.), insurance, and small businesses. It's a 30-year plus life history of combined experience. I also learned from great mentors. I feel privileged. It's now time to share all this with others and give my contribution to the betterment of other people's lives.

I also realized that because of over-specialization, folks in the financial markets camp did not know much about real estate investing, and folks in the real estate camp knew next to nothing about investing in financial markets. And even less people have ever tried buying and running a small business. Finally, almost no one knows how to efficiently set up a whole life insurance policy for estate planning and OPM/I to boost all other investments. Therefore, I decided to write new books in the format of Modules to teach how-to concepts and ideas, along with sharing my real-life experiences and secrets learned on the battlefield:

- Module 1 – *Accelerate with* **Money Booster: Optimize Use of Money**
- Module 2 – *Accelerate with* **Real Estate Investing**
- Module 3 – *Accelerate with* **Financial Markets**
- Module 4 – *Accelerate with* **Autorun Small Business**

Since I'm still writing them at the moment this book is published, I decided to give you, my dear reader, three things as a **free BONUS** for reading my book:

1. **A recorded video on each of the 4 Modules.** They will cover essential contents of the books. The videos can be found in my author website. To effectively help more people, I will start from the basics assuming you are a novice in the field and start building up from there. You will learn how to get started with each particular instrument covered, be it real estate, stock market, etc., to help you in your implementation of the AFFF.
2. **A special workshop:** Introduction to the Accelerated Financial Freedom Formula™, where I will explain the basic concepts of the method and the FlightPlan in a recorded video format to watch at your convenience.
3. **A special booklet on Asset Protection, Risk Management, and Tax Optimization.** You will be able to download it in PDF.

→ **How to get all these BONUSES:** Go to my author website, register, get a login, and you will get access to all the materials available for download, including but not limited to:

- My view on the Economy and the Stock/Bond/Real Estate Markets (updated regularly)
- The four Modules in video format
- Additional instructional videos on specific topics
- Tools in Excel spreadsheets
- How-to checklists in PDF
- Book previews on future books to be launched
- New editions of published books, new chapters, improvements, and corrections
- And more…

For more information, please refer to Chapter 11 – Next Steps.

To conclude, I will just make a brief introduction of each of the four Modules. But make sure you get access and watch the videos. It's free. I spent many hours making them especially for you, to help in your financial freedom journey because I know there is so much to learn. And quickly! I'm sure this material will be helpful for you.

Module 1 - Money Booster: Learn how to optimize use of money to get more bang for your buck

I discussed the concept of OPM/I several times in previous chapters, especially when I described the 3rd and the 4th principles of the AFFF:

- Principle #3 – **Other People's Money Leveraging Your Investments**
- Principle #4 – **Money Boosters (Optimization of Money)**

I also listed the 8 pillars that make up the 4th principle of the AFFF:

1. The Time Value of Money: often neglected in favor of higher returns, time can be just as powerful.
2. The Magic of Compound Interest.
3. The Real Cost of Interrupting Compound Interest.
4. The Lost Opportunity Cost: you finance everything you buy. Even cash has a cost.
5. The 10 Wealth Eroding Factors. Procrastination itself is one: every day counts.
6. Fix Your Money Leaks even before you think about saving money.
7. Focus on Volume of Interest, instead of Interest Rates.
8. Borrow Other People's Money to Invest: Pay interest on a declining principal (by amortization) and earn interest on an increasing principal (by compounding interest).

I also introduced some of the basic ideas and concepts behind some of the pillars. But there is a LOT more! In the video and the new book, I will discuss the OPM/I concept, how to create it, how to use it to leverage other investments, each of the above topics in more detail, and a lot more.

Watch **Module 1 –** ***Accelerate with*** **OPM/I Money Boosters** video to learn more at my author website.

Module 2 - Real Estate Investing: Why it is a goldmine for accelerating your financial freedom

Real estate is probably the best asset for income generation purposes for most people. I know it's a strong statement, but it is true. That may be why it's so popular among financial freedom seekers. Besides income generation, real estate also delivers strong capital appreciation over the long-term and is a very tax-advantaged asset class. The downsides, critics often point out, are low liquidity (relative to financial assets) and the amount of work involved dealing with tenants and maintenance. I know these things scare a lot of people away. However, these downsides are mostly associated with physical real estate investments. When I'm referring to real estate, it's in a broader sense, extending much beyond single-family homes (the most popular), multi-family apartments, or commercial buildings. In case you're not familiar, there are also other forms of real estate investments that don't involve dealing with physical structures, tenants, or toilets. We are going to discuss the following forms of real estate investments:

- Single-Family Home
- Multi-Family Building (under and over 4 units)
- Commercial Real Estate
- Deeds of Trust (Mortgage Note): "The Paper Real Estate Investing"
- Real Estate Syndication
- Real Estate Crowdfunding

As you will learn, each of these different ways to invest in real estate shares the same basic income generation engine. Each modality will have pros and cons and may offer a better fit for different investor personalities. Single-Family Homes and Small Multi-Family buildings (under 4 units) are the easiest ways for new investors to get started. Over time, you will realize, they are not optimal for scale. Then you should move up to large Multi-Family buildings. To make this transition, you will need to learn a lot more about specifics of Multi-Family investing because it is not just size that changes. But if you are an investor who cannot wrap your head around dealing with "tenants & toilets," which is perfectly understandable, you may want to consider investing in "paper assets" backed by real estate. For example, Deeds of Trust or Mortgage Notes let you invest in real estate and receive income without dealing with tenants, management, repairs or maintenance. And if you want to be more passive as an investor because you really don't have the time, you may want to consider investing in a syndication or even crowdfunding. Here, you would join as a passive, limited liability partner. You provide the capital together with other investors, and the sponsor of the real estate project will manage the project for a fee. In other words, there are so many available options for you to invest in real estate in various ways, shapes, or forms.

If you never considered investing in real estate, for whatever reason, or you have just never had the chance before, this is the moment to rethink your existing beliefs. Maybe you invested before and ran into big problems, like I did. Or perhaps, you may have heard horror stories from others. But whatever has been your prior experience, you must know that in anything we do in life – from practicing sports to studying for an exam, and to making investments, any type of investments – sometimes we succeed, sometimes we fail. It's normal; it's life. The best way to tip the balance overwhelmingly towards success is proper education. The more you learn and experiment with baby steps initially, the more proficient you will become and achieve success. Real estate made so many people millionaires; there is really no reason for you not to do well investing in real estate.

Why do I say real estate investing is a goldmine you shouldn't miss? I will discuss each one of these unique advantages of real estate investing in greater detail, but let me just list them for now:

- Income generation engine that can provide a stable, long-term source of cashflow.
- Appreciation that can be forced by you even if the market doesn't "cooperate."
- One of the very few assets that can be recession-proof. This is big!
- Real asset that provides hedge against inflation.
- There is not one national real estate market; it's fragmented in thousands of regions and localities with their own cycle dynamics, unlike centralized markets like the stock market.
- Tax advantage: depreciation "phantom" expense to save on taxes.
- Tax advantage: classification as passive income by the IRS with tax rates that can be zero.
- Tax advantage: indefinitely defer capital gains taxes to build your real estate empire.
- Your tenants pay your mortgage, and over the long run, they buy the properties for you.
- There are many types of investments from which to choose, from the most active to the most hands-off.
- You can use a self-directed IRA or a self-directed 401k to invest in real estate.
- The best one of all: the OPM/E and OPM/I boosters work best with real estate.

The net result of all these advantages is that you will get the income you need to sustain your financial freedom. It is actually an impressive list of advantages unique to the asset class, not easily found in other investment asset alternatives.

Watch **Module 2 –** ***Accelerate with*** **Real Estate Investments** video to learn more at my author website.

Module 3 - Financial Markets: Learn how to tame risks to accelerate your journey to Financial Freedom

Stock investing is very risky, right? Just like most folks who primarily invest in real estate, I find it amazing the number of people who disdain, hate, or are simply scared of investing in the stock market. I can understand why in most cases, though. They may have had bad experiences (a.k.a. lost money or knew others who did), or they were simply told to stay away from the stock market. Well, I was one of those telling folks to stay away from the stock market if they didn't know exactly what they were doing and/or they didn't have a reliable risk management system. But most people who don't invest in stocks say they are simply afraid of losses, or they don't have enough knowledge to successfully invest in stocks. And they are right. I still tell folks to stay away from the stock market if they don't know what they are doing.

Stock investing can indeed be very risky, but only if you do it the wrong way, which is what the majority of non-professional investors do, unfortunately. There are many right ways to invest in stocks; some ways are better than others, and your choice will depend on your own style, your personal circumstances and goals. We will discuss this in more detail, but first, let me explain and convince you why you do want stocks in your journey to financial freedom.

Stock investing can really help you accelerate your financial freedom journey. Bull markets can speed up your capital formation much faster than fixed income alternatives (e.g. CD, savings, bonds, etc.). Look at this chart showing the spectacular growth stocks delivered to investors over the years. It would be a pity (a sacrilege!) to simply let go of this fantastic opportunity.

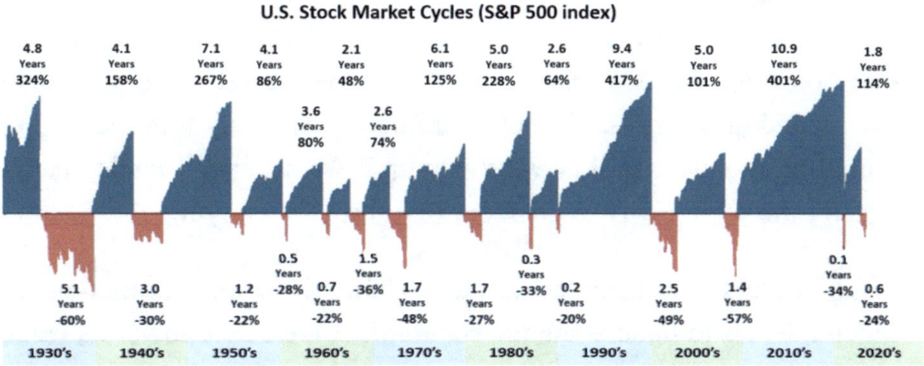

But what about the risks that inevitably come with high returns? This is exactly why I always say that you must have a reliable risk management system when you invest in stocks. The problem with most stock investors is that they don't. Often, they believe they do, but in reality they don't have the discipline to make hard decisions and often end up making the worst decisions in critical times. A reliable risk management system designed for successful stock market investing can be achieved through proper education.

Like everything else in life, there is the right way and the wrong way to invest in the stock market. When I first started, I did it the wrong way, obviously. I was pretty much just following the crowd. I was young, I heard people bragging about the money they were making in the stock market, and I jumped right in, expecting to make a quick buck. As I did more and more, the only consistent thing happening was that I was losing all the time. So hurt, I decided to stop and never do it ever again. Looking back, it is obvious why I had failed. I wasn't properly educated, and I didn't even know what risk management really meant. Today, I see people jumping on the crypto bandwagon. I see these folks are making the exact same mistakes I made in my youth. Worse, in fact, because unlike stocks that have real companies producing wealth behind them, cryptocurrencies are based on nothing but the faith they will be worth more tomorrow than today. So, I ask these people: how do you manage your risks? How do you know the fair price of a cryptocurrency? The answer to my first question often is, "No, risks are not really managed." The answer to my second question is, "I think more people will buy it in the future; therefore, the price will *certainly* go up." Wow… my friends, that is exactly the wrong way to go about investing… in anything!

The right way to invest in the stock market (and any market for that matter) is to understand the economic drivers that power its value appreciation. Understand why stock prices are going up. Why they go down. You also need to understand what the risk factors are that may derail your investing plans. Then you need to create a system to guide you and to keep risks under a tight control.

Believe me, after decades of investing in multiple financial markets (stocks, bonds, currencies, interest rates, even electricity) and real estate markets, I have learned that to be minimally successful, you must be willing to learn how to do it like a professional. Yes, you heard me right. I said, "…like a professional," or in a professional manner with seriousness. If you invest (in anything) like an amateur, you will get typical amateur results. I'm sorry to say that, but it is what it is; I don't make the rules. Now, you may be thinking, "But how about letting professionals take care of my investing for me?" This is an alternative, but still, you should be the decision maker. I think it's a very bad idea to rely on others to make important decisions on our behalf. Investment decisions are one such type of important decision. I think we should outsource execution to third parties to do it for us, but never important decisions. That is why I strongly believe we should be proficient in stock market investing so that we can make smart decisions confidently, even if we hire someone to execute orders for us. For you, on the road to financial freedom, it is even more crucial to get your own financial education and total control over your finances. You really won't want others in the driver's seat leading something so important in your life. It is not difficult, believe me. We are all capable of learning. We just need to invest some time and set our minds to it.

Watch **Module 3 –** ***Accelerate with*** **Financial Markets** video to learn more at my author website.

Module 4 - Autorun Small Business: Learn how to invest in a small business to super-speed up your journey

Before you quickly dismiss this Module just because it might look impossible to you, or "This is not for me," just give me a chance to explain how a small business that runs essentially without you is not only very possible but also not as hard as you may be thinking. Keep reading, and if you are skeptical beforehand, I believe this may change your mind. If done right, this may really accelerate your journey to financial freedom.

If you have been a real estate investor, you will have a nice surprise: you will find that running a small business is quite similar to running a real estate investing business. The transition will not be very hard. Here, you also screen deals, perform due diligence, make offers, negotiate with the seller or the seller's brokers, set up an LLC, manage the business and the income statement, etc. There are differences, of course, but a real estate investor is halfway there.

The best news about investing in a small business is its return on investment (ROI) or the income stream it generates in relation to the investment amount required.

It is often possible for small businesses to return an ROI in the high double digits.

If financed, it may reach triple digits.

In my mind, this is true because there are much less people chasing small businesses than real estate. People are easily discouraged for no reason other than some preconceived idea that small businesses go bankrupt all the time. While many do, millions of small businesses remain in business for decades. Ownership changes, but the business is still up and running for generations. Just look around you.

Bear in mind that **I'm not talking about starting a new business. I'm talking about acquiring an existing business** with all its systems already set up and running smoothly. **Starting a business from scratch is where most of the risk is concentrated.** It's also very hard to start up a business because you will have to figure out everything. When you buy a business, you are actually not only buying its income generation power (a future stream of income), but also the systems someone had already set up, its existing customers, suppliers, employees, assets, orders, inventory, etc. Acquiring a business is generally easier, safer, and smarter than starting one, especially if your goal is financial freedom, not to be a business tycoon someday.

But can we find a niche in the small business space:

- A small business that is safe and easy to operate
- A small business that allows an absentee owner
- A small business that is already profitable but with potential for further improvement
- A small business with a good structure, team, management, and finances
- A small business that has a double-digit ROI even without leverage, which can be further leveraged

Just to be clear, I'm indeed talking about a real business, not side hustles! Many in the FIRE community often talk about adding side hustles to increase your income, if not too laborious or time-consuming (ideally passive) and ideally something you are good at or passionate about. While side hustles may be helpful, they bring in very little money and will not help much with materially shortening your journey to financial freedom. If you want to accelerate your financial freedom, you need to think bigger. It's math; not an opinion. You will need a real business, one that can produce a double or even triple-digit ROI.

On your journey to financial freedom, the first thing you need is income generated from your investments that can replace your earned income through work where you trade your time for money. But wait – Running a business is hard… It's nothing like investing in the stock market or in real estate… It's too much work… Too much risk… I hate dealing with employees… I don't have capital to start… I have no experience… It's unrealistic for me! – Yes, I hear you and I feel your pain. I was in your shoes and had the same thoughts. Even friends and family tried to discourage me. Nevertheless, if so many people around the world succeeded, why shouldn't we? We all know what we need to do: obtain proper education for things we still need to know, such as learning how to find a small business that fits our criteria and how to run it profitably. I hope I can help you with both. In the end, you will notice it's not as hard as you had thought or what other people (especially those who have never done it) are telling you to scare you off.

And yes, I did say **"autorun."** Let me define what I mean by "autorun." You probably guessed it. Autorun means it that it runs by itself. In other words, it's a business that ideally runs without you, or at least, with a minimal requirement for your own intervention in day-to-day activities. You said "ideally," so it's not realistic, right? Nope, it can be done, and many entrepreneurs were able to do it. The secret is that you must buy the business with this in mind already. The numbers of the business you are looking to buy must generate enough revenue to afford hiring a manager to take your place. Again, you retain decision making on all important and strategic matters of the business, but you delegate the day-to-day operation of the business to the manager and your employees. But is this possible? Very. I know of restaurants where the owner stops by only once a day (or every few days) to write checks and see if all is well. Ten to fifteen minutes in the restaurant and he is gone. I know of laundromats that operate automatically. Robots are already making pizzas in vending machines. With increasing technology, more opportunities like these are emerging.

But if you say, "Hey, I want 100% passive investing," then this is not it. A 100% passive investment is either a myth or delivers subpar results. There will always be some work involved. Real estate investing is not 100% passive. Even stock investing requires time and effort (unless you want to invest like an amateur and lose money or delegate to someone else to deliver underperforming results to you). The reality is that all the best things in life require effort. If you want to be lazy and adopt a totally hands off approach to investing, you will invariably achieve poor results, below your potential. And forget about achieving financial freedom fast. If you are serious about accelerating your financial freedom, you should invest at least some time and effort into it.

I believe an autorun small business is a fantastic asset class for investors who want to step up their game above and beyond real estate and stock investing. The ROI is truly amazing, and done right, it will seriously abbreviate your journey to financial freedom. If you are feeling unsure and not confident, you only need one thing: proper education to learn more and acquire experience. I believe I can help you take the first steps.

Watch the **Module 4 –** ***Accelerate with*** **Autorun Small Business** video to learn more at my author website.

As we come to the conclusion of this chapter, let me emphasize again that the content has been recorded in videos. I invite you to register at my author website and watch the videos. It's free for purchasers of this book as a bonus. All you need to do is to enter the coupon code **SMARTCHOICE** during checkout, that prices will become zero for you.

The content will also be made available in **my next books** to be published in a series:

The AFFF Collection Series

- Module 1 – *Accelerate with* **Money Booster: Optimize Use of Money**
- Module 2 – *Accelerate with* **Real Estate Investments**
- Module 3 – *Accelerate with* **Financial Markets**
- Module 4 – *Accelerate with* **Autorun Small Business**

Don't miss out! 🙂

CHAPTER 10

10. Execution, Final Thoughts, and Gratitude

Execution: Implementation of your own AFFF Flightplan and Launch

In any plan that gets tangible results, learning and strategy are just the beginning, the planning phase. The second phase will be the execution. Here is where projects often fail; so let's dedicate due attention to it. Like Mike Tyson used to say, "*Everybody has a plan until they get punched in the mouth.*" The devil is in the details of the execution. For example, you decided to invest in real estate only to find out later that you can't get a mortgage loan because you don't have strong credit. Or you made a plan with life insurance but later found out you were uninsurable because you have a serious health condition. Or you invested in stocks right before a bear market hit and you got stuck in a losing position. These are all situations that can happen to anyone and make a formidable challenge or even a roadblock to any plan. That's another reason you need all weapons available to you in case your chosen ones fail. Your strategy must be strong enough to give you options in case you face headwinds. Believe me, you will. All of us will face difficulties and challenges at some point in our journeys. But this does not mean we should give up on our dreams. We must be flexible, smart, and open-minded to make necessary adjustments. The challenges should make us stronger, wiser, and more focused on the ultimate prize at the end of the journey. My goal is to help you get there… but also faster, and if possible, a lot faster!

Financial freedom is a really big deal, believe me. It will make your life so much easier, instead of worrying about money all the time. You will be free to say "goodbye" to that toxic work environment, if you happen to work in one not because you want to, but because you needed the money. You will have so many new possibilities in life open up for you, some of which you have never even considered before, when you are financially free.

The secret is determination and learning quickly what to do and how to do it. Don't be afraid of trying new things you have never done before. Remember the opening story in the Introduction of the Book about Albert Einstein? It is a lesson that teaches us that we can only get extraordinary results if we do extraordinary things. Sitting on a couch watching TV all day or working hard for your employer but letting someone else decide how to invest your money won't get you extraordinary results. That is just the reality. Look around you. No one has your best interests at heart other than yourself, always remember that. To get results you never got before, there is only one way: you have to do things you have never done before.

I know that not everyone was blessed the way I was in terms of exposure and opportunity to learn and experience multiple markets. I was afforded the chance to fail early and fail often. These experiences forged my learning. It would be arrogance and lack of empathy on my part to judge other people's fears about doing something for which they might have reservations. That is okay. We overcome obstacles by studying and learning more about them. The more we learn, and concepts start to make sense in our brains, the less anxious and concerned we become. Knowledge is power. My goal is to empower you with knowledge and show you the way. That is precisely why I'm producing more educational content through videos, workshops, and even mentorships. At least you won't make the same mistakes I made!

I want you not just to read my books, but I want you to put the knowledge into practice and achieve your financial freedom.

To help you with your execution, this book alone will not be sufficient (I can't condense everything you need to know here) unless you already have plenty of experience investing in financial markets, real estate, small business, and whole life insurance. Very few people might. Most people have experience investing in some of the above but not all of them. And some people have never done any of the above, and that is okay. People come from different walks of life. Whatever your case, I encourage you to tour my author website. I'm working hard to produce educational content appropriate to everyone at every skill level, especially beginners. I'm sure you will find the help you need to execute your AFFF Flightplan all the way to financial freedom.

As I said earlier in the book, I developed the AFFF independently from mainstream ideas about how to reach financial freedom. I only learned about the FIRE movement, the 4% Rule, etc., even the name "Financial Freedom" or "Financial Independence," very late, after I had already started grouping and organizing the four AFFF principles. In my mind, I was only seeking a way to "early retirement," because I had been bullied at work for years, and I started looking for a definitive solution for me. But the fact of the matter is that I realized the financial expert community was really not doing a great job helping people achieve financial freedom. In my view, the mainstream methods were so inefficient that you can see the evidence here if you pause to think about it:

- Why do financial experts speak of retirement planning all the time but rarely talk about **early** retirement (before age 65) or financial freedom?

- What is the recommended minimum amount you need to save to retire? You can read financial columns or just do a Google search. Financial pundits often talk about $3 million, $5 million, always in the order of millions. Even for retiring on bare minimums, it is about $1 million. In other words, only millionaires can afford to retire without worry, nowadays? How about everyone else?
- For everyone else, the prescription generally is work really hard, get new sources of income from side hustles, and save aggressively. Live extremely frugally, well below your means for years and decades, to save and invest in tax-deferred plans (401k, IRA, etc.) managed by big firms, investing your money in stocks, bonds, mutual funds, etc. and charging nice fees. Then, if and when you become a millionaire like those mentioned above, you will win your financial freedom and can retire like them.

I think these three things are clear evidence that the methods are very inefficient. They are not bad, just so inefficient that it can only effectively help those who are already at the top of the income and wealth ladder. My eureka moment came when I asked a simple question: would the method I was developing for myself over the years (yes, it did not have a name, nor was it one concise "method" at that time; it was just a bunch of ideas and lessons learned in my mind) that employed multiple asset types work better? I was also already using other resources; e.g., market timing, OPM, and even learning how to use several money strategies to get the most bang for my hard-earned buck. In time, I organized all this knowledge into a method, and I called it the Accelerated Financial Freedom Formula™ (or simply, AFFF) and decided to write this book.

In conclusion, I would like to congratulate you on reading this book, and especially for taking your personal financial matters so seriously. If you are here, it says a lot about you. I really want to see you succeed. I want to hear your success story. You will face headwinds in your journey, and I wish to hear your stories about overcoming challenges, too. You can send me your story by email (sidney@shauy.com). Our stories can always help and inspire others if you allow me to share them with others (anonymously if you like). Now, after reading the book, it is time to take action! Take the first step, baby steps if necessary or if you are too busy. Just don't drop the ball. Start the journey today. Learning and planning are part of the journey too. In a sense, you have already started the journey!

In Chapter 8, you have a 9-STEP Checklist to start your journey to financial freedom today, without delay. Remember that TIME is your most valuable asset and also that time and money are synonyms. Don't delay your financial freedom unnecessarily by procrastination. The AFFF is all about speed. If you felt attracted to read this book in the first place, it is because you want to accelerate your way to financial freedom. So, join in the movement and let's keep moving!

If you feel fully capable to DIY your AFFF plan, by all means, go ahead, and I wish you the best of luck! If you feel you need help, do reach out to me through my author website, participate in our workshop activities, read my newsletter, take online courses on specific topics you might need, or enroll in our mentorship programs. The goal is clear. We want you to succeed in pursuing and achieving your own financial freedom… and FAST!

Final Words of Gratitude

I hope I was able to meet your expectations when you set out to read this book. My goal was to challenge your existing beliefs by offering an alternative solution outside mainstream sources. Writing the book took me months, but I hope I was able to deliver real value to you. I also hope you will be able to make good use of what you learned here to transform your life, reaching the dream of financial freedom.

I would like to offer my words of gratitude for your trust. After "speaking" so much, now I wish to hear what you have to say. I only ask you to leave me your honest assessment as feedback to help me improve myself as an author and communicator. I truly value what you think! I would very much appreciate an honest review on Amazon:

https://www.Amazon.com/review/create-review?&asin=B0C3X94R25

Your input will guide my next steps to create better content, make changes, improve, and better help everyone.

Thank you!

Sidney Shauy, MBA

CHAPTER 11

11. Next Steps: Claim your Free Bonus Package (and more!)

FIRST, CLAIM YOUR FREE BONUSES! – Get from my Author Website

The Bonus Package – *Free with Coupon in the Book*

Video content

- **Module 1:** *Accelerate with* Money Boosters: Optimize Use of Money
- **Module 2:** *Accelerate with* Real Estate Investments
- **Module 3:** *Accelerate with* Stock Market
- **Module 4:** *Accelerate with* Autorun Small Business
- **Special Workshop:** Introduction to the Accelerated Financial Freedom Formula™
- **Special Booklet:** Asset Protection, Risk Management, and Tax Optimization

Downloads

- **Excel spreadsheet:** FlightPlan Simulator.xlsx
- **Excel spreadsheet:** FlightPlan Simulator for Examples Used in the Book.xlsx
- **Excel spreadsheet:** Real estate simple pro-forma template.xlsx

- **PDF file:** The Self-Assessment Questionnaire.pdf
- **PDF file:** The 9-Step Checklist of the Accelerated Financial Freedom Formula™

Note: New free materials may be added; visit us often. Use the coupon code **SMARTCHOICE** during Checkout, and prices will go away. These BONUSES are exclusive for those who purchased the book.

New Editions of the Book: Free for Life! You will be eligible to receive the e-book version of any new editions of this book should they be launched. You will also receive updates to the current edition, including erratum and corrections. You must be registered with your email to receive my free newsletter (below) to be notified.

Free Newsletter: By registering your email during checkout, you will automatically sign up for my free newsletter. You can opt-out at any time. I will periodically include some of my market analysis, opinions, and other related content. You will also receive notifications

Earn Money by Referring Friends: If you enjoyed the book and learned from me, you can be my partner and earn commissions just by referring the book to friends, family, and others who you believe would also benefit from it! Just sign up for my Affiliate Program and start earning commissions!

* * *

Mentorship Programs and Live Workshops – A more interactive experience

Mentorship is designed to be a key part of the learning process to accelerate learning and achievement of important implementation milestones of a project. My mentorship is recommended for everyone who wants closer assistance implementing their financial freedom plan with a more interactive experience. I will coach you every step of the way to achieve specific targets. Mentees will have immediate access to all the educational material (recorded videos, checklists, guides, spreadsheets, etc.). Live sessions with the author, Sidney Shauy, are held on a weekly basis (will be recorded). The goal is to help you get off the ground and implement your plan. Live Q&A, and you can also ask me questions offline by email. Some examples of mentorship programs offered include (check them out in my author website; titles are subject to change and new titles will be introduced):

Financial Freedom Destination – Goal: Achieve your 1st milestone: Basic Financial Freedom

Financial Markets Plus – Goal: Become a sharp financial markets investor

Multifamily Real Estate (Workshop) – Goal: From zero to your 1st deal as a multifamily investor

Real Estate Notes (Workshop) – Goal: Screen, analyze, and buy your 1st real estate notes

* * *

Video Courses and Recorded Workshops – *On-demand in my author website*

I strive to offer a variety of courses covering multiple types of assets for beginners and advanced investors alike because everyone's needs are different. Each course was carefully designed with a single purpose in mind: to take you from wherever you are today, at least a few steps closer to your financial freedom.

On-demand online courses and recorded workshops were also designed to be convenient for everyone to learn concepts quickly, especially those who lead very busy lives. They are also priced inexpensively, so everyone can access and take advantage of getting great educational value in return for their money. Some examples of on-demand video-courses and recorded workshops include (titles are subject to change and new titles will be introduced from time to time):

Financial Markets --

Stock Market Investing Made Simple: Take 1st Steps to Profit Without Fear (for beginners)

How to Create a 95% Automated Stock Investing System (for all the busy people out there!)

Double Your Gains But Not Your Risks (learn how to explore the PD/M2x concept in action)

Beat the S&P 500: Build an Easy-to-Execute System (a comprehensive approach)

Real Estate --

Get Started: Find, Analyze, Negotiate, and Buy Your First Single-Family Home Investment

Get Started: Find, Analyze, Negotiate, and Buy Your First Multi-Family Investment

The Most Passive Real Estate Income Machine (Learn how to invest in real estate notes)

6 Steps to 6-Digit Income from Real Estate Investments (A complete blueprint)

Autorun Small Business --

Double-Digit ROI Cashflow Machine (Explore a semi-passive alternative with higher ROI)

Monetize Your Brain (Share your expertise and passion with others and monetize it)

Money Boosters --

From Pennies to Millions: 8 Money Strategies to Get the Most Bang for Your Buck (Explore strategies to make your money really work for you)

* * *

The Freedom Seeker Member Community – *Free Trial*

As a member of this Community, you will get:

- Weekly updates on my **view** on the economy, the stock market, and the real estate market
- Daily commentary on the stock market plus lessons how to interpret data
- Webinars to teach strategies involving multiple assets, e.g., stocks and real estate with insurance to achieve higher returns, lower risks, income stability, etc.
- Webinars about topics of interest for special situations, e.g., what to do if you have credit card debt, families with special needs individuals, etc.
- Priority previews of new training programs under development, including books
- Special priority discounts for new books and other eligible materials by the author
- Share your own stories and words of wisdom with the community. Hear feedback, grow, and travel together toward financial freedom.

Membership for the Community is free to all until further notice. When it becomes paid, the cost will be symbolic, just to help us properly maintain it. The goal is to deliver value and help people achieve financial freedom. Sign up at the author website.

* * *

The Accelerated Financial Freedom Formula™ Book Collection Series

- **Module 1:** Money Boosters – Optimize Use of Money
- **Module 2:** Real Estate
- **Module 3:** Stock Market
- **Module 4:** Autorun Small Business

Coming soon! You will be notified of the publication dates of the new books if you register your email at my author website when you get your free bonuses.

CHAPTER 12

12. Frequently Asked Questions (FAQ)

a) Does the AFFF work? Why?

The AFFF works for a simple, easy to understand reason. First, it is not a product, a service, nor an investment, but a method. Methods are good or bad compared to other methods. In Chapter 6, you can read about the mathematical proof for why the AFFF does what it is designed to do – **accelerate your journey to financial freedom** – compared to mainstream traditional methods. Second, millions of people around the world have achieved financial freedom one way or another with less powerful methods. Therefore, if traditional methods worked for so many people, a superior method would work even better. That's the logic. For "better," I want it to translate to faster results.

The goal of the AFFF is to help you **achieve financial freedom faster with less money required** than mainstream traditional methods. I demonstrated throughout the book that the 4 principles can make a huge difference in terms of accelerating your journey to financial freedom compared to methods that don't employ all these features.

I gave you a mathematical proof. We discussed at length in Chapter 6 why a mathematical proof is superior compared to a user testimony because it is objective truth. Testimony is based on individual experience, and it is anecdotal evidence or subjective truth.

b) Would the AFFF work for ME?

For the same reasons above. A method works or it doesn't. I proved it does, so there is no reason it should not work for you.

For whom might the AFFF not work? I think the problem, which is not related to the method, *per se*, would be for folks who belong to subsets from the general population that cannot implement the AFFF for one reason or another. For example, if someone is precluded from getting a mortgage or buying a whole life insurance policy, he/she would lose the power of OPM. Another situation would be someone who makes an extremely low income or is unable to save much, if any money, in a way that even the acceleration provided by the AFFF is still not enough for them to achieve financial freedom in their lifetime or in a reasonable number of years. This may be the case for a subset of the population, unfortunately. Again, the AFFF is designed to accelerate the journey, but 10 x 0 is still zero, or 10x a very small speed still may be a small speed, and that is not the fault of the method; it's just math.

Except for extreme cases like these, if these are not your life circumstances, there is really no clear reason why the AFFF shouldn't be able to accelerate your journey to financial freedom.

c) I'm not sure I will be able to implement the AFFF. I don't have the time / the money / the discipline / the motivation / the skills (knowledge) / or all the above and more.

These are all valid concerns. Before taking on a project, we have to make a self-assessment to know ourselves and travel mentally to project into the future we wish to achieve but also imagine the journey itself. Most people tend to give up even before trying if they perceive obstacles in the way, which may be unreasonably magnified from reality. Self-doubt causes fear and paralysis. We often believe we aren't capable of doing things when in fact we are fully capable; we just don't know because we have not yet tried.

The AFFF was designed to fit the needs of most people, even those with the following concerns:

I'm afraid to invest; I'm too conservative as an investor: Sure, the AFFF is a multi-asset method: just pick the assets that suit you best with the lowest risks. Your journey will be slower, but that's okay because it is your own pace and in your comfort zone.

I'm too impatient; may I speed up my journey even faster? Pick assets with the highest ROI within your risk tolerance.

I'm too busy, I have no time for this: Some people are extremely busy with their career and life; I get that. But shortage of time should really be no reason to deny yourself the realization of a dreamed financial freedom if it is important to you. You need to realize that **financial freedom is all about getting your time back!** It is true that you will have to make an initial investment of time, money, and effort to implement the AFFF. But you will be able to get out of the rat race by trading your time for money when you achieve financial freedom. The good news is that the AFFF was designed to be **flexible enough to help people with little time** still be able to accomplish their goals. For example, in Stage I, Outperform signals take less than 5 minutes a day to follow and execute. In Stage II, if you don't want to be a landlord, I get that. But there are many ways around it. You can invest in real estate syndication projects, for example, where you invest passively. So, yes, if you really have almost no time at all, the AFFF is flexible enough to help you, too, achieve your financial freedom and essentially get your time back.

I'm not disciplined enough to follow a recipe: You may be feeling this way because of past frustrations and failures with some other methods. The truth is that we all experience setbacks. I certainly did have my fair share of failures and disappointments in life. But remember that every project is different. There is no reason this project would fail if you had failed before with other projects. Discipline is a learned skill. You can cultivate it and get better and better every day. Some people are disciplined enough to execute a step-by-step plan on their own while others will feel it's harder and will need help. It's natural and perfectly normal. For these folks who feel they lack the discipline, they may be helped by a mentorship. They may find it helpful to have individualized attention that gives them the rhythm and pace to keep themselves on task and motivated to take each step along the journey. They may also benefit from belonging to a community with others seeking the same goal on the same journey. I do offer a mentorship program to help people implement the AFFF and a community of like-minded financial freedom seekers as part of the financial education component.

I'm not sure I'm motivated enough: If you are reading this book, I'm sure you are motivated. You may *feel* you are not motivated to take the next step, though. The reasons for such a feeling may be many. For one, you are not yet fully convinced of the method. If that's you, it's okay. You can do a small trial and see the results for yourself before jumping whole body into it. Wait until you are fully convinced if that helps. Other folks may feel unmotivated because they haven't seen why financial freedom could be so important in their lives. If that is you, learn more about what financial freedom is all about. Read other books from many different authors on the same topic, if that helps.

I'm just too lazy to do this; I rarely check on my investments; I prefer simple rules of thumb or just leave all my finances to my banker or advisor: Unfortunately, this is the reality for a lot of people, including white-collar college-educated professionals. They focus so much on their careers, making themselves busy all the time making money, that they neglect their own investments, delegating to someone else to manage for them. Deep down, they realize what they are doing is far from optimal, but they do it anyway for the sake of convenience and to avoid the hurdle of change. Deep down, they know that simplistic and static rules of thumb are just too simplistic in a complex world to really work. Deep down, they know they should be properly educated in personal finance and be in charge of their own finances. Most bankers and financial advisors are good people and experts in their fields, who can be great allies to help you achieve your financial goals. However, you should always be the boss. If you don't know enough finance to direct your advisors and make the final decisions, you need to get financial education. This way, you help them help you. Wall Street made things so easy and convenient for us to just outsource our own responsibilities to someone else to care for us. Unfortunately, like my grandpa used to say, no one will have your best interests at heart except yourself. Think about it. Why did a lot of near-retirement folks lose so much money in their rigid 401k accounts during the 2008 financial crisis and were forced to work longer and delay retirement age as a result? Why the market crash still destroyed their retirement funds? Remember that few things in life, if any, are great and worthy and can be achieved without effort. In life, everything seems to have a cost to pay, one way or another. Often, you pay for poor decisions in life at the highest cost you aren't even aware of. This is one such decision. By outsourcing to a 3rd party something as important and valuable as your own financial life and future, you may feel you are getting a good deal. Yes, you free yourself from the worries or lack of financial education for a reasonable fee (sometimes not so much) and get time back to do anything else while your hired specialist deals with everything. But in the long run, money leaks, opportunity costs are lost, and sub-optimal decisions will accumulate, often without you even knowing. Your hard-earned money could have earned you much more, but you forfeited for convenience. Think about it. For your own sake. You may have done this for so long that any change feels like huge, insurmountable hurdles. Change is always hard, I know. But the good news is that the AFFF is there to help you. I can help with your financial freedom and even offer mentorship with individual attention if you need. Note that mentorship is not "done for you" but education. You will learn how to manage your bankers and advisors, with you seated in the boss' chair, fully aware of your financial situation, and pushing your specialists to work their best for you. This is because knowledge will empower you.

I have no money! This is classic. It is often just an excuse masking other reasons because money is a matter of priority. I understand that some people earn minimum wage and can't really save much for the future. Others endure heavy expense burdens, including debts due to life circumstances and also are not able to save much. I hope this situation will be temporary and that they will be able to improve their livelihoods given time, perhaps with education and/or entrepreneurship. But for those who are not in such hardships, where they put their money is a matter of choice. If financial freedom is an attractive enough destination for you, you should give it the highest priority. Also, the AFFF is designed so the money required for its implementation is sharply reduced by the use of OPM. The AFFF also strives to accelerate your savings growth in Stage I, which seriously helps those with less financial resources. In other words, a higher ROI makes a small investment grow to the get same results as a lower ROI on a larger investment. Again, the AFFF was designed to help folks with less means and low saving rates as well.

I don't have the skills or knowledge required: Hey, this is exactly why the AFFF was developed in the first place. More than a method, the AFFF is financial education. By learning the AFFF method, you will actually be learning finance and investments! For those who think they are "too old" to learn, remember we are learning all lifelong. We never stop learning. It's imperative for older adults to keep learning every day to keep their minds sharp, so there is no excuse for not learning new skills at any age. Besides this book, I also offer online courses on specific topics, workshops, and even a mentorship for those who require a more individualized attention to help them learn and implement the AFFF in their lives to achieve financial freedom faster and with less money required, while learning about real estate, the stock market, life insurance, how to read economic indicators, how to make good financial decisions, etc. Remember that no one is born with skills; all skills and knowledge are learned and experienced in life. Like my mom used to say, knowledge is the most valuable asset no one can ever take away from you. Load yourself with knowledge and learn new skills every day.

d) My retirement savings are entirely invested in 401k and IRA's. Should I withdraw and invest elsewhere?

This is a common question because, given the popularity of tax-deferred retirement plans (or qualified plans), most people, including myself, invested heavily in these accounts. I can't really answer for you, because withdrawing large amounts will invariably generate taxes and possibly penalties, but I can talk about my views on this. I offered my opinions on qualified plans in Chapter 8, STEP 8, about tax optimization. I took a long time but finally realized I would be better investing my hard-earned money elsewhere. I learned that most schemes that are mass distributed to the public at large are rarely great things, to be honest. Tax deferral seemed like a great deal on the surface. But tax deferral is not tax free. You will still be taxed at the tax rates prevailing at the time of withdrawals. What would happen if tax rates increased in the future, right when you reach retirement age and start taking withdrawals? With government debt skyrocketing and a social security that doesn't inspire a solid confidence, do you think tax rates are more likely to increase or decrease in the future? This is the main reason I decided not to invest anymore and also to downsize my 401k and IRA accounts over the years, paying taxes and even penalties, to invest the money elsewhere. But that is me. You will have to look at your own situation to make a decision. Everyone's circumstances are different and unique (age, amount invested, goals, etc.).

e) My personal savings rate has dropped year after year because my wage increases can't keep up with inflation. What can I do? Give up on my dreams of ever becoming financially free?

Unfortunately, this is a real situation going on in this country. Personal savings are declining fast, not only because personal income hasn't had real gains for decades, but inflation was reborn and interest rates spiked. More people are doing more side hustles to make ends meet. That underscores the importance of financial freedom in a person's life. If your assets were working to produce income for you,

you would be less exposed to risks of declining income from work or even unemployment. For those who haven't started their financial freedom journey, it's a wake-up call. If this is you and you want to get started on your financial freedom journey, but you are afraid you might not be able to save much, don't despair. The most important thing is to recognize you have a problem. That is the first step towards any solution. The top priority for anyone barely getting by is survival. Make sure your expenses are paid and avoid making debt, if possible. It may be hard for some time, but as soon as things improve a little, you should be able to start saving again. Life is a struggle for most of us. What will determine our fate is our determination to succeed and a little luck. So, don't give up on your dream. Work hard to make it a reality.

f) What is the best time to start whole life insurance policies?

Mathematically speaking, we should always start as soon as possible. The reason is very simple. The cost of insurance grows with the age a person starts his/her policy. Even 1 year older, you would statistically have a higher probability of death than your own younger self. That is because mortality risk increases with age. However, a whole life insurance policy's premium is determined at the time you start the policy, and it stays fixed and will never change, even though you may be paying a smaller amount over a very long time. Therefore, the earlier you start, the better. What if you can't afford it? You can always start small. There is one reason you may want to delay your start, and that is your impatience to accelerate your financial freedom. In this case, you may want to skip funding whole life for OPM/I at the beginning of your journey. That is understandable. But also think about the journey as a whole. Remember that while whole life might not help with the speed of your journey initially, but it will add stability to it and accelerate it towards the destination later on. If you want to stop money leaks, create OPM/I to leverage your assets, prepare for retirement, and leave a legacy for your kids, it may make sense to start sooner rather than later. Often, the rabbit may travel fast initially, but it is the turtle who wins the race.

g) What if I can't qualify for a mortgage?

This may happen to many people for a lot of different reasons. Not everyone has spotless credit reports with 700+ credit scores. Some people may not be US residents or not have the proper documentation and get denied a mortgage loan. What to do then? Fortunately, our spaceship has two boosters – the OPM/E and the OPM/I. If one of them fails, we have another. If you can't obtain a mortgage, OPM/E failed. In this case, you still can leverage your assets but only with OPM/I. That's why the "I" stands for internal. It's because the decision to get leverage doesn't depend on others (the External for "E" in OPM/E). If you had funded a whole life insurance policy earlier, you would have cash value built into your policy and would be able to use it as collateral for a policy loan. That's another good reason I believe we should always start whole life policies as early as possible. It takes time for the cash value to grow, so it has to be started early. If you want OPM/I to work for you and you haven't even started a single policy, you will have to wait perhaps a few years until cash value has accumulated enough money and earnings. The good news of OPM/I is that it doesn't depend on your credit report or someone else approving or denying you for credit. If you have cash value in your whole life policy, the insurance company will always finance you, often up to 95% of your cash value.

Now, is there a chance you might be denied life insurance too? The vast majority of people won't have a problem qualifying for life insurance. However, unfortunately, some people with certain health conditions or engaged in activities considered high risk, will be denied. What do you do if this happens to you? You can work on your finances to get your credit in order for OPM/E. It may take some time, but eventually you should be able to achieve it.

h) Can I implement the AFFF even if I don't feel confident in managing my own finances?

Confidence comes from having the right set of knowledge and skills, which in turn comes from proper financial education. If you are not confident managing your own financial affairs or your finances are upside down, you are not alone, and it may not have been your fault. The education system was designed decades ago with the aim to produce workers for industry and services, not investors, financially savvy people, and entrepreneurs. Many folks in my generation and even after mine grew up getting traditional education with little to no emphasis towards financial education. I was lucky because I worked in the financial industry. But when I graduated from engineering school, I knew next to nothing about finance. In summary, there is really no substitute for education. Often people knowing little about finance buy products and services that aren't appropriate for what they really need. These products and services often don't match what each person really needs. Therefore, I think financial education should be your focus and priority in life because it is just way too important to be relegated to the back seat. Get your education and you will feel confident, making good decisions for your own future.

i) I'm "allergic" to stocks. Can I implement the AFFF without stocks?

While stocks are a great instrument for capital appreciation, especially during Stage I, to accelerate your financial freedom journey, I understand that many people simply cannot tolerate the risks. The mere daily fluctuations may make very conservative people nervous. That is not healthy and should be avoided. However, if this is you, before you give up the entire asset class, consider this alternative. As presented in Chapter 5, the Outperform project may provide a suitable alternative. Outperform Level I is a low-cost subscription service that will help you participate in the S&P 500's rallies while avoiding risky moments by staying in cash during times of turmoil. Level I's goal is not to eliminate all market fluctuations entirely but to warn you to avoid major corrections and crashes the market may experience from time to time. If you still want to stay out of the stock market as an asset class entirely, you can. You can implement the AFFF entirely without stocks. Your travel speed may not be as fast as it could be with stocks, but that is up to you. So, the answer to this question is yes. Not optimal, but yes.

j) I don't think I can tolerate tenants & toilets. Can I implement the AFFF without real estate?

As I said throughout the book, real estate is an essential component of the AFFF, but yes, you can achieve your financial freedom with the AFFF without real estate. An alternative to real estate, another asset class that can be leverageable is a small business. But I suspect that people who don't like real estate often don't see themselves running a small business, even if it's mostly run by a hired manager. Some people are allergic to employees, and I can understand that as well. But before you cross real estate or a small business off your list of asset choices, I want you to think creatively, out of the box. As you can see in Module 2 – *Accelerate with* Real Estate Investments (information how to download the contents in Chapter 9), there are many ways to invest in real estate without having to deal with tenants and toilets. One very easy and really passive way to invest in real estate is investing in a real estate syndicated project. You would participate with capital alongside other investors who are passive members of the LLC that own the project. The management responsibilities lie with the sponsors or managers of the investment syndication. There is also crowdfunding, REITS, and private equity that work similarly, and you won't have to deal with tenants and toilets and can still invest in real estate. Another alternative is real estate notes, especially the performing type of notes. As you can see, there are alternatives to consider before giving up the asset class completely. But again, the choice is yours. Without real estate and a small business, you may be killing Stage II, because of the inability to leverage with OPM/E. But if you have sufficient cash value in your whole life insurance policies, you may alternatively count on OPM/I.

k) Real estate investing and small business are too laborious for me. I want to be completely passive. May I?

Yes, you may. But remember that effort pays off, and things that require some effort will almost always outperform things that require little effort, especially in the long run. The laziest approach to investing is buy and hold an asset for the long run, which often means that you have no clue or a plan to ever sell it. It's a little like wait and see. Unfortunately, a lot of people do this thinking they would do well just holding stocks for the long run because stocks (and home prices) *always* appreciate, which is not true. Some other people want to be so passive and believe they can do well just by outsourcing their entire financial lives to someone else to deal with it. While this attitude may help you live life as usual and may even perhaps lead you to your financial freedom eventually, it is far from optimal and invariably will take a very long time to get there. In summary, if financial freedom is important to you, treat it as such. Invest in your own financial education and make an initial effort to build your assets. They will take you somewhere you have never been before. I'm sure it's well worth the effort. Finally, if you want to achieve financial freedom with the minimum effort possible under the AFFF, you may choose Outperform Level I or II (it only takes 5 minutes or less per day of your time) for Stage I and invest in a real estate syndication as a passive investor (virtually no effort at all on your part) in Stage II.

l) I have no money to spend on financial education. May I implement the AFFF with this book alone?

Yes, you can, especially if you already have some experience with stock market investing (I mean experience with at least more gains than losses) and with real estate. If this is you, read the entire book to understand the concepts and principles well and just follow the step-by-step formula to implement the AFFF. If you are finding it difficult to do so, it's a sign you may need to improve your financial education or may need more personalized attention. To make it easy for you, I will offer a few options ranging from online courses and workshops on specific topics to enrich your understanding and skills for a price I'm sure you can afford (just check it out on my author website). For those who need a closer helping hand, I will offer a mentorship program.

m) I want to start investing today but ALL markets are falling. There are talks of a coming recession. Should I invest in something, and what, or just sit and wait?

This is a very important question many investors are asking, especially in 2022 and early 2023, because the context is very challenging. In good times, a rising tide lifts all boats, and any investment will probably turn out well enough and everyone seems to be a genius; but in bad times, a falling tide will require much more of your skills and cleverness. While there is no silver bullet and every situation is different (no two recessions are alike), there are some ways to navigate a pessimistic scenario where apparently nothing seems like a clear, good option. Let's take the stock market and real estate, for example. Assume both markets are not very encouraging at the moment. You want to start implementing your AFFF today. What should you do? Sit and wait for the markets to turn? While this is certainly an option but generally not a good one because time is money and you don't want to delay your financial freedom, it may be the best option, depending on the circumstances. To help you decide, let me offer some pointers. This is the kind of situation that I cannot give you the fish, but I can teach you how to fish. I will teach you how to think in a situation like this, which you should likely encounter in your journey. Remember that all markets have cycles, and the size of the cycles is different for each market and type of asset. First, consider the type of asset. The stock market fluctuates a lot faster than real estate. Stock prices are based on future expectations. As soon as expectations change, stock prices change immediately in response. Therefore, the stock market will find the bottom much earlier than real estate. The window of opportunity to ride the next bull market will come earlier in the stock market. But real estate also has its advantages during hard times. Remember that the residential sector of real estate, especially multi-family rentals, tends to fare well during recessions. Also, the real estate market is very fragmented. The duration of cycles varies from a coastal city to an interior city, a large metro area to suburbs, etc., and at any given time, you will find sub-markets at different points in the cycle. Therefore, you will pretty much always have options in real estate to start investing. It is a matter of searching where the hidden opportunities are. In Module 2 – *Accelerate with* Real Estate

Investments (see Chapter 9), I discuss how you can do your research to find emerging markets at favorable points in the cycle for you to jump right in. In stressful times, when confidence is low, tangible assets like gold and precious metals tend to do well. There are options if you think multi-asset. Now you can clearly see the advantage of having a multi-asset approach vs. a single asset. Again, unlike in good times, in bad times, you need to be much better at what you do. Some people say "survival of the fittest;" I won't go that far, but you get the idea. Second, note that even during bear markets in the stock market, you can still make profits with what's called "bear market retracements" or "bear market rallies". This can be very lucrative with short-term gains, but it's not for the novice stock market investor because you would need to be timing the market very closely. If you get timing right, you can make quick profits, but you can easily lose money as well. One alternative is to subscribe to Outperform's live signal (see box in Chapter 5) to help you do it. There are other ways to navigate troubled waters when the markets are challenging, trending in a direction that does not favor us investing at the moment. I gave you a few ideas to help you think and strategize your own solutions.

n) Some people say we must be specialists in one single asset type (e.g., real estate, etc.) to do it really well because we will become a "jack of all trades, master of none", if we embrace multiple types of assets. Is it true?

Nope, not at all. This may be only true for those with narrow minds. I, myself, and many people I know, who are versed in multiple markets, are the perfect counter-examples. Is the person telling you this a specialist? Think about this: - Do you play (or enjoy) only one single sport? I bet you play at least a few, which is normal. If you have the ability to play more than one sport, you have the ability to learn and invest in more than one asset. It's as simple as that. As to the advantage of learning deeper about one asset if you focus on it, it is true. By focusing on one, you will certainly learn that one really well. However, after learning up to a certain point, further incremental gains will start to produce smaller and smaller marginal benefits. This happens with anything we learn, doesn't it? Thus, you must find the best balance for you. For me, it's abundantly clear that I'd better invest my time learning multiple assets reasonably well than focusing all my time in one single asset to become a specialist in it. Besides losing the ability to explore opportunities that arise in other more promising markets by focusing on a single one, thereby underperforming my full potential, I really don't think it's a smart idea to be over-dependent on one single market. As explained in the book, there are so many external factors I don't control, which can wreak havoc my financial freedom plan, that having multiple choices may also turn out to be a lifesaver.

o) I have questions not addressed here. May I contact you to ask?

Yes, you sure can. Register at my author website to get your bonus content and support materials. Send me a message through my website or you may also email my support team. I will answer all serious questions and inquiries at my earliest convenience. www.acceleratedfinancialfreedom.com

If you have comments and suggestions, please kindly leave me your honest reviews on Amazon with a testimonial. They will be very appreciated and help me improve myself as an author to better help everyone. I do care about what you have to say and I will read every single review. Here is the link for your convenience:

https://www.Amazon.com/review/create-review?&asin=B0C3X94R25

APPENDIX

*** Self-Assessment Questionnaire**

*** FlightPlan Simulator Results for Bob, Aline, Mario, and Ting**

SELF-ASSESSMENT QUESTIONNAIRE

PART I – *Self-Knowledge*

1) Why is financial freedom important to me? How motivated I'm in its pursuit?

2) What are my dreams? What is my vision for a successful and happy life without financial worries?

3) Where am I today, and where do I want to go? What do you want to achieve?

4) Am I mentally prepared to start this journey?

5) Am I able to do it by myself, or do I need help? Are there areas I need more education?

PART II – *Personal Circumstances*

6) How is your current financial life? Are you happy? What is your current income? Is it sufficient to cover all your current expenses? How much can you save every month?

7) What types of income sources do you have (e.g., wages, commissions, tips, rental income, etc.)? Is your income steady and stable, or does it fluctuate in unpredictable (or hard to manage) ways?

8) Do you have personal challenges to consider? Family issues? Debt? Long-term dependents to care for? Is there anything holding me back from working toward my dreams?

9) How much time per day (or per week) can you set apart to dedicate to implementing your AFFF Flightplan?

10) Can you make a projection of your future income needs based on information and plans you already have today (e.g., children going to college, weddings, home purchases, new babies, etc.)?

PART III – *Investor Profile*

11) When you engage in a new project or make a new investment, what is your level of anxiety expecting to see its results?

    (a) I'm pretty laid back. I know it may need time to work. I'm patient to wait for the best results, even if it takes slightly longer than expected.
    (b) I'm impatient and want to see results as fast as possible.
    (c) I'm somewhat patient.
    (d) I'm somewhat impatient.
    (e) I'm right in the middle.

12) If an investment you made is losing money, what would you likely do?

    (a) Unless losses are too significant and the scenario too unfavorable, I would keep investing because I know that losses can happen in the quest for gains.
    (b) I would be very disappointed but not give up investing.
    (c) I would never invest anymore.

13) You consider yourself:

    (a) A very conservative investor.
    (b) A somewhat conservative investor.
    (c) A somewhat aggressive investor.
    (d) A very aggressive investor.

14) What asset types are you most comfortable with investing in:
    (Mark your answers with: V = Very comfortable, C = Comfortable, N = Not comfortable)

(a) Stocks, stock indexes, ETFs, stock funds
(b) Bonds, annuities, and other fixed-income securities
(c) Real estate – residential (single family)
(d) Real estate – residential (multi-family)
(e) Real estate – commercial
(f) Real estate – notes
(g) Real estate – syndication (passive investing with a professional portfolio manager)
(h) Whole life insurance
(i) Small business professionally managed by a hired manager

15) What asset types are you most proficient or experienced with investing:
    (Mark your answers with: E = Expert, K = Very knowledgeable, N = Know nothing)

(a) Stocks, stock indexes, ETFs, stock funds
(b) Bonds, annuities, and other fixed-income securities
(c) Real estate – residential (single family)
(d) Real estate – residential (multi-family)
(e) Real estate – commercial
(f) Real estate – notes
(g) Real estate – syndication (passive investing with a professional portfolio manager)

(h) Whole life insurance
(i) Small business professionally managed by a hired manager

PART IV – *Financials*

16) List below your income and expenses (your personal/family income statement):

Income source	Amount	Frequency	Remarks
Total Income			

Expense	Amount	Frequency	Remarks
Total Expense			

NET INCOME	

(Net Income = Total Income – Total Expense)

Add lines as needed. Use monthly or annual figures, whichever fits your situation best.

17) What assets and liabilities do you have right now (your balance sheet)? Fill the table below with your financial information:

Asset	**Value**	**Liquid?**	**Where (e.g., bank X, etc.)**
Savings account			
CD			
Stocks, ETFs			
Bonds			
Mutual funds			
401k			
IRA			
College plans			
Life insurance			
Personal residence			
Investment properties			

Businesses			
Total Assets			

Liabilities	**Value**	**Due**	**Where (e.g., bank X, etc.)**
Mortgages			
Credit cards			
Student loans			
Car loans			

Total Liabilities			

18) What is your current credit score? Are there derogatory items (e.g., unresolved accounts in collection, bankruptcy, etc.) that may prevent you from obtaining a mortgage on an investment property?

19) Do you have life insurance? Please list all policies you have: (Type: term life, whole life, or universal life.)

Life insurance policy	**Cash value**	**Death benefit**	**Premium**	**Type**
Total				

20) Do you have liability insurance (umbrella policy)? Amounts? Are all your properties adequately insured?

Flightplans for Bob, Aline, Mario, Ting

BOB'S FLIGHTPLAN

FLIGHTPLAN SIMULATION FOR: **BOB**

SAVINGS SIDE	Annually	monthly
Savings rate	0	0
Current savings	500,000	
Baseline	7.86%	Historical 60/40 (Base)
Asset 1	11.80%	Outperform Level I
Asset 2	30.10%	Outperform Level II

Year	Baseline	Asset 1	Asset 2
	7.86%	11.80%	30.10%
0	500,000	500,000	500,000
1	539,300	559,000	650,500
2	581,689	624,962	846,301
3	627,410	698,708	1,101,037
4	676,724	781,155	1,432,449
5	729,915	873,331	1,863,616
6	787,286	976,384	2,424,565
7	849,167	1,091,598	3,154,359
8	915,911	1,220,406	4,103,821
9	987,902	1,364,414	5,339,071
10	1,065,551	1,525,415	
11	1,149,303	1,705,414	
12	1,239,638	1,906,653	
13	1,337,074	2,131,638	
14	1,442,168	2,383,171	
15	1,555,522	2,664,385	
16	1,677,786	2,978,783	
17	1,809,660	3,330,279	
18	1,951,900	3,723,252	
19	2,105,319	4,162,596	
20	2,270,797	4,653,782	
21	2,449,282		
22	2,641,795		
23	2,849,440		
24	3,073,406		
25	3,314,976		
26	3,575,533		
27	3,856,570		
28	4,159,697		
29	4,486,649		

INVESTMENT SIDE

Target Income	**300,000**

I. Real Estate Investing (Own $)	
Cap rate	7%
Unleveraged Return	7.0%
Asset size	4,285,714
Target Capital	**4,285,714**
Monthly income	**25,000**
Annual income	**300,000**

II. Real Estate Investing + OPM/E	
Cap rate	7%
Loan rate	3%
Tenor (years)	30
LTV	80%
Leveraged Return	14.6%
Asset size	10,279,397
Target Capital	**2,055,879**
Req. money reduction	**48.0%**
Speed increase	**2.1x**
Monthly income	**25,000**
Annual income	**300,000**

III. Autorun Small Business (Own $)	
Multiple (2x - 3x ODI)	3.0x
Price for acquisition	900,000
Annual net return	33.3%
Target Capital	**900,000**
Monthly income	**25,000**
Annual income	**300,000**

IV. Autorun Small Business + OPM/I	
Loan rate	8%
Tenor (years)	5
LTV	60%
Leveraged Return	45.8%
Asset size	1,638,812
Target Capital	**655,525**
Req. money reduction	**72.8%**
Speed increase	**1.4x**
Monthly income	**25,000**
Annual income	**300,000**

SPEEDOMETER

	RE Income Engine		**ASBuz Income Engine**		
	RE Own $	**RE OPM/E**	**ASB Own $**	**ASB + OPM/E**	
Target Capital -->	4,285,714	2,055,879	900,000	655,525	
Historical 60/40	29	19	8	4	years
Outperform Level I	20	13	6	3	years
Outperform Level I	9	6	3	2	years
Historical 60/40	1.0x (base)	1.6x	3.8x	7.5x	
Outperform Level I	1.5x	2.3x	5.0x	10.0x	
Outperform Level I	3.3x	5.0x	10.0x	15.0x	

4% Rule

Target Capital	7,500,000	
Reduction	-73%	-91%
Year to reach	30	
(with 60/40 BP)		

ALINE'S FLIGHTPLAN

FLIGHTPLAN SIMULATION FOR: **ALINE**

SAVINGS SIDE	Annually	monthly
Savings rate	18,000	1,500
Current savings	200,000	
Baseline	7.86%	Historical 60/40 (Base)
Asset 1	11.80%	Outperform Level I
Asset 2	30.10%	Outperform Level II

Year	Baseline	Asset 1	Asset 2
	7.86%	11.80%	30.10%
0	200,000	200,000	200,000
1	234,427	242,662	280,909
2	271,561	290,358	386,172
3	311,613	343,682	523,118
4	354,813	403,299	701,286
5	401,409	469,950	933,082
6	451,667	544,466	1,234,649
7	505,875	627,775	1,626,987
8	564,344	720,915	2,137,419
9	627,409	825,045	2,801,491
10	695,431	941,462	3,665,449
11	768,799	1,071,617	
12	847,934	1,217,129	
13	933,290	1,379,813	
14	1,025,353	1,561,692	
15	1,124,654	1,765,034	
16	1,231,759	1,992,370	
17	1,347,282	2,246,532	
18	1,471,886	2,530,685	
19	1,606,284	2,848,367	
20	1,751,245	3,203,537	
21	1,907,601	3,600,616	
22	2,076,245		
23	2,258,146		
24	2,454,343		
25	2,665,962		
26	2,894,214		
27	3,140,407		
28	3,405,950		
29	3,692,365		

INVESTMENT SIDE

Target Income	**250,000**

I. Real Estate Investing (Own $)

Cap rate	7%
Unleveraged Return	7.0%
Asset size	3,571,429
Target Capital	**3,571,429**
Monthly income	**20,833**
Annual income	**250,000**

II. Real Estate Investing + OPM/E

Cap rate	7%
Loan rate	3%
Tenor (years)	30
LTV	80%
Leveraged Return	14.6%
Asset size	8,566,164
Target Capital	**1,713,233**
Req. money reduction	**48.0%**
Speed increase	**2.1x**
Monthly income	**20,833**
Annual income	**250,000**

III. Autorun Small Business (Own $)

Multiple (2x - 3x ODI)	3.0x
Price for acquisition	750,000
Annual net return	33.3%
Target Capital	**750,000**
Monthly income	**20,833**
Annual income	**250,000**

IV. Autorun Small Business + OPM/I

Loan rate	8%
Tenor (years)	5
LTV	60%
Leveraged Return	45.8%
Asset size	1,365,676
Target Capital	**546,271**
Req. money reduction	**72.8%**
Speed increase	**1.4x**
Monthly income	**20,833**
Annual income	**250,000**

SPEEDOMETER

	RE Income Engine		**ASBuz Income Engine**		
	RE Own $	**RE OPM/E**	**ASB Own $**	**ASB + OPM/E**	
Target Capital -->	3,571,429	1,713,233	750,000	546,271	
Historical 60/40	29	20	11	8	years
Outperform Level I	21	15	9	7	years
Outperform Level I	10	8	5	4	years
Historical 60/40	1.0x (base)	1.5x	2.7x	3.8x	
Outperform Level I	1.4x	2.0x	3.3x	4.3x	
Outperform Level I	3.0x	3.8x	6.0x	7.5x	

4% Rule

Target Capital	6,250,000	
Reduction	-73%	-91%
Year to reach	30	
(with 60/40 BP)		

MARIO'S FLIGHTPLAN

FLIGHTPLAN SIMULATION FOR: **MARIO**

SAVINGS SIDE	Annually	monthly
Savings rate	12,000	1,000
Current savings	0	
Baseline	7.86%	Historical 60/40 (Base)
Asset 1	11.80%	Outperform Level I
Asset 2	30.10%	Outperform Level II

Year	Baseline	Asset 1	Asset 2
	7.86%	11.80%	30.10%
0	0	0	0
1	12,472	12,708	13,806
2	25,923	26,916	31,768
3	40,433	42,800	55,136
4	56,082	60,558	85,537
5	72,962	80,412	125,090
6	91,168	102,608	176,548
7	110,806	127,424	243,496
8	131,987	155,168	330,594
9	154,832	186,186	443,908
10	179,474	220,864	591,331
11	206,052	259,634	783,127
12	234,719	302,979	1,032,655
13	265,640	351,438	1,357,290
14	298,991	405,616	1,779,640
15	334,963	466,187	
16	373,763	533,905	
17	415,612	609,613	
18	460,751	694,256	
19	509,438	788,886	
20	561,951	894,682	
21	618,592	1,012,963	
22	679,685	1,145,201	
23	745,580	1,293,042	
24	816,654	1,458,329	
25	893,314		
26	976,001		
27	1,065,186		
28	1,161,381		
29	1,265,137		
30	1,377,048		
31	1,497,756		

INVESTMENT SIDE

Target Income	**100,000**

I. Real Estate Investing (Own $)	
Cap rate	7%
Unleveraged Return	7.0%
Asset size	1,428,571
Target Capital	**1,428,571**
Monthly income	**8,333**
Annual income	**100,000**

II. Real Estate Investing + OPM/E	
Cap rate	7%
Loan rate	3%
Tenor (years)	30
LTV	80%
Leveraged Return	14.6%
Asset size	3,426,466
Target Capital	**685,293**
Req. money reduction	**48.0%**
Speed increase	**2.1x**
Monthly income	**8,333**
Annual income	**100,000**

III. Autorun Small Business (Own $)	
Multiple (2x - 3x ODI)	3.0x
Price for acquisition	300,000
Annual net return	33.3%
Target Capital	**300,000**
Monthly income	**8,333**
Annual income	**100,000**

IV. Autorun Small Business + OPM/I	
Loan rate	8%
Tenor (years)	5
LTV	60%
Leveraged Return	45.8%
Asset size	546,271
Target Capital	**218,508**
Req. money reduction	**72.8%**
Speed increase	**1.4x**
Monthly income	**8,333**
Annual income	**100,000**

SPEEDOMETER

	RE Income Engine		ASBuz Income Engine		
	RE Own $	RE OPM/E	ASB Own $	ASB + OPM/E	
Target Capital -->	1,428,571	685,293	300,000	218,508	
Historical 60/40	31	23	15	12	years
Outperform Level I	24	18	12	10	years
Outperform Level I	14	11	8	7	years
Historical 60/40	1.0x (base)	1.4x	2.1x	2.7x	
Outperform Level I	1.3x	1.8x	2.7x	3.2x	
Outperform Level I	2.3x	2.9x	4.0x	4.6x	

4% Rule

Target Capital	2,500,000	
Reduction	-73%	-91%
Year to reach	32	
(with 60/40 BP)		

TING'S FLIGHTPLAN

FLIGHTPLAN SIMULATION FOR: **TING**

SAVINGS SIDE	Annually	monthly
Savings rate	6,000	500
Current savings	0	
Baseline	7.86%	Historical 60/40 (Base)
Asset 1	11.80%	Outperform Level I
Asset 2	30.10%	Outperform Level II

Year	Baseline	Asset 1	Asset 2
	7.86%	11.80%	30.10%
0	0	0	0
1	6,236	6,354	6,903
2	12,962	13,458	15,884
3	20,216	21,400	27,568
4	28,041	30,279	42,769
5	36,481	40,206	62,545
6	45,584	51,304	88,274
7	55,403	63,712	121,748
8	65,993	77,584	165,297
9	77,416	93,093	221,954
10	89,737	110,432	295,665
11	103,026	129,817	391,564
12	117,360	151,489	516,327
13	132,820	175,719	678,645
14	149,495	202,808	889,820
15	167,482	233,093	
16	186,881	266,952	
17	207,806	304,807	
18	230,375	347,128	
19	254,719	394,443	
20	280,975	447,341	
21	309,296	506,482	
22	339,842	572,600	
23	372,790	646,521	
24	408,327	729,165	
25	446,657	821,560	
26	488,000	924,858	
27	532,593		
28	580,690		
29	632,569		
30	688,524		
31	748,878		
32	813,976		
33	884,190		

INVESTMENT SIDE

Target Income	**60,000**

I. Real Estate Investing (Own $)

Cap rate	7%
Unleveraged Return	7.0%
Asset size	857,143
Target Capital	**857,143**
Monthly income	**5,000**
Annual income	**60,000**

II. Real Estate Investing + OPM/E

Cap rate	7%
Loan rate	3%
Tenor (years)	30
LTV	80%
Leveraged Return	14.6%
Asset size	2,055,879
Target Capital	**411,176**
Req. money reduction	**48.0%**
Speed increase	**2.1x**
Monthly income	**5,000**
Annual income	**60,000**

III. Autorun Small Business (Own $)

Multiple (2x - 3x ODI)	3.0x
Price for acquisition	180,000
Annual net return	33.3%
Target Capital	**180,000**
Monthly income	**5,000**
Annual income	**60,000**

IV. Autorun Small Business + OPM/I

Loan rate	8%
Tenor (years)	5
LTV	60%
Leveraged Return	45.8%
Asset size	327,762
Target Capital	**131,105**
Req. money reduction	**72.8%**
Speed increase	**1.4x**
Monthly income	**5,000**
Annual income	**60,000**

SPEEDOMETER

	RE Income Engine		**ASBuz Income Engine**		
	RE Own $	**RE OPM/E**	**ASB Own $**	**ASB + OPM/E**	
Target Capital -->	857,143	411,176	180,000	131,105	
Historical 60/40	33	25	16	13	years
Outperform Level I	26	20	14	12	years
Outperform Level I	14	12	9	8	years
Historical 60/40	1.0x (base)	1.4x	2.1x	2.6x	
Outperform Level I	1.3x	1.7x	2.4x	2.8x	
Outperform Level I	2.4x	2.8x	3.8x	4.3x	

4% Rule

Target Capital	1,500,000	
Reduction	-73%	-91%
Year to reach	34	
(with 60/40 BP)		

Meet the Author

Sidney Shauy is an analytics-driven investor and entrepreneur, who designed solutions combining financial instruments, real estate, and insurance. With over 30 years of combined experience with financial markets, real estate investing, and insurance structuring, the author writes a daily market commentary, analysis, opinions, and related topics on Medium and also runs the Outperform (renamed RISP 500™) algorithm on the S&P 500 index with a team of market veterans. In real estate, Sidney managed multi-family investments for a syndication group of investors and invested in deed of trust notes. He also designed insurance structures to boost returns and lower risks, working in conjunction with other investments.

Sidney serves as SME (Subject Matter Expert) on a per project basis for the Banking Division of a renowned global consulting firm. Previously, Sidney worked 20+ years in leading international banks such as Citigroup, Morgan Stanley, Lloyds Bank, ABN Amro, Bilbao Vizcaya, and in some of the most important financial centers in the world, such as New York, Hong Kong, and Sao Paulo (Brazil). Sidney has experienced multiple financial crises since the early 1990's while successfully managing several billion-dollar portfolios at risk for his employers. He also developed a number of quantitative methods for risk management, pricing for financial derivatives, and financial engineered solutions.

Sidney earned an MBA degree from the Wharton School of the University of Pennsylvania and an engineering degree from Escola Politecnica of the University of Sao Paulo in Brazil. He was also an exchange student with Insead in Fontainebleau, France and obtained a mathematics in finance certificate (non-degree) for the Master of Science program from the Courant Institute of Mathematical Sciences at New York University.

Sidney lives in the New York City metro area with his wife, son, and a lab dog called Cadie. He loves science fiction movies, stories, and science books, especially about theoretical physics.

SIDNEY SHAUY

Financial Freedom Accelerated 2x-10x

https://engineering-finance.medium.com

https://www.linkedin.com/in/sidneyshauy/

https://www.acceleratedfinancialfreedom.com/

Check our website: www.acceleratedfinancialfreedom.com

COMING SOON! (EXPECTED MAY 2023)

THE BONUS PACKAGE

100% FREE FOR PURCHASERS OF THE BOOK

Use the COUPON CODE inside the Book to watch the videos and download the support materials

The Coupon Code can be found in Chapters 9 and 11 of the Book

Special Workshop (Bonus): Introduction to the Accelerated Financial Freedom Formula

Course

Module 1 (Bonus): Accelerate with Money Boosters: Optimize Use of Money

Course

Module 2 (Bonus): Accelerate with Real Estate Investments

Course

Module 3 (Bonus): Accelerate with Financial Markets

Course

Module 4 (Bonus): Accelerate with Autorun Small Business

Course

Special Booklet PDF (Bonus): Asset Protection, Risk Management, Tax Optimization

Download

Excel Spreadsheet (Bonus): Flightplan Simulator

Download

Download the FlightPlan Simulator in Excel to simulate your own financial freedom plan.

PDF (Bonus): The Self-Assessment Questionnaire

Download

Know yourself, reflect on your wants, and set your unique vision and goals. This is the first step of your journey toward financial freedom.

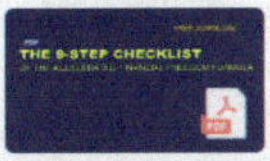

PDF (Bonus): The 9-STEP Checklist of the Accelerated Financial Freedom Formula

Download

Use the 9-Step Checklist to help you plan your path to financial freedom.

COMING SOON! (EXPECTED MAY 2023)

MENTORSHIP PROGRAMS

Group coaching, 1-on-1 premium mentorship, live workshops

COMING SOON! (EXPECTED MAY 2023)

VIDEO COURSES AND WORKSHOPS

Convenient on-demand online courses and recorded workshops

Made in United States
Cleveland, OH
06 November 2026

47771492R00144